CITIZENSHIP

CITIZENSHIP

Paul Barry Clarke

Pluto  Press

LONDON • BOULDER, COLORADO

First published 1994 by Pluto Press
345 Archway Road, London N6 5AA
and 5500 Central Avenue, Boulder, CO 80301, USA

British Library Cataloguing in Publication Data
A catalogue record for this book is available from the British Library

Library of Congress Cataloging in Publication Data
Citizenship / Paul Barry Clarke
190pp. 24cm.
Includes bibliographical references
ISBN 0-7453-0585-7 (hbk) – 0-7453-0586-5 (pbk)
1. Citizenship. I. Clarke, Paul Barry, 1946-
JF800.C58 1993
323.6–dc20   93-29326
                                                      CIP
ISBN 0 7453 0585 7 hbk.
ISBN 0 7453 0586 5 pbk.

Designed, typeset and produced for Pluto Press by
Chase Production Services, Chipping Norton
Printed in Finland by WSOY

Contents

Part I

Citizen Human

Citizen Human

Human beings describe themselves, and understand themselves, in numerous ways. They are men, women, persons, selves, subjects, individuals, mothers, fathers, children, brothers, sisters, members of ethnic groups, of religious groups, of national groups and even, in some cases, citizens.

As human beings mutually describe and perceive themselves so, in significant ways they are. Their own self-descriptions, reinforced by, or challenged by, others, are central to their self-identity, to their perception of their self; of their self-worth. Little wonder then that humans cling to and often elevate one or other of these aspects of their identity and place it in a central position in their life. In an individualised, some would say over-individualised, age such tendencies can be both prevalent and dangerously divisive.

Our age is one of emerging nationalist claims, emerging ethnic claims, social heterogeneity, and new social movements. Recognition and self-determination are sought by peoples in a way not seen hitherto. The collapse of the Soviet Union and its eastern European satellites has produced new civil societies and new challenges for its peoples. The break-up of apartheid, and of changes in the kind of rule in South Africa, requires the formation of new political identities for substantial numbers of its people. Europe and North America face the challenges of migration, of ghettoisation, of multi-culturalism, of particularism. People describe themselves and are described in various ways. These descriptions, the associated activities, practices and inter-reflection upon these descriptions, activities and practices constitute Being.

There are many ways of partial being. One may partially be a man, a woman, a person, a self, a subject, an individual, a mother, a father, a child, a brother, a sister, a member of an ethnic group, a religious group or a national group. One may even partially be ... a citizen. Of all the categories available to humans it is only the latter that is exclusively, solely and fully political. All the other ways of partial being may involve, or overlap with, the political – they may even be required for it, or emerge from it – but none are exclusively concerned with human being as political Being.

Yet this, the political figure of Being, being a citizen, which is apparently one of the most partial and specific modes of Being, turns out to be fundamental; for where a full, rich concept of citizenship is lacking politics is absent, in abeyance, hiding, side-tracked, or even suppressed. Where citizenship and politics are absent the project of Being human is itself side-tracked.

The idea of Being, as including being a citizen, is both culturally specific and historically persistent. In some ways it is more persistent than some of the other ways in which we understand ourselves. The idea of the self emerged as a consequence of the inward turn generated in Christian thinking. The individual, understood as an autonomous being having an inherent value, emerged as a consequence of, on the one hand, the breakdown of the great chain of being, the feudal order, and, on the other hand, the rise of Protestant thinking with its direct appeal to God.

The related idea of the person as a moral being and as a metaphysical category was similarly an idea late in developing. Just as these ideas are historically specific so they, and their cognate notions, are culturally specific. Not all peoples have understood their form of Being as being a self, an individual, a subject, or as a citizen. As there have been many and varied forms of life so there have been many and varied forms of human Being. By contrast, western forms of life, and some of their predecessor cultures, have persistently thrown up forms of Being that carry some idea, albeit inadequately expressed and practised, of common status with respect to the regulation of society.

Before Politics

The word 'citizen', derived from *civitas*, is distinctively Latin in origin. However, the idea of citizenship, understood as active membership of and participation in a body politic, is generally regarded as emerging first in Greece at about 600–700 BC. It is usually taken that a necessary condition for the emergence of this conception of the citizen was the development of the *polis*, the Greek city-state. This distinctive form of political community was able to provide economic conditions which freed some people from the particularities of their own immediate needs. From such freedom from necessity emerged the idea of a mode of being in which a number of people could direct their attention to matters of general concern.

Ideas which underlie this early emergence of the concept of citizenship and which still persist, albeit in different ways, within the concept, are those of equality and freedom. The components of these ideas pre-date Hellenistic culture and are found in embryonic form in some of its predecessors. The earliest known reference to an abstract concept of equality is found in a text of about 2000 BC when the writer has it that God (the All Lord) made the winds so that, 'every man might breathe ... like his fellow ... [He] ... made the inundation that the poor man might have rights like the great man ... [and] he ... made every man like his fellow ...' [1]

The ideas of equality and freedom have some expression prior to the emergence of Greece from its own earliest times. However, it is in that emerging culture that these ideas were developed and given a political significance. Some form of the Greek language seems to have existed about 1500 BC but the earliest written references to the *polis*, understood then as denoting a town, occur about 700–800 BC. Homer uses the word *polis* to refer to a fortified town; at that time the notion of the political and the notion of the citizen seem to exist only in the most embryonic form.

The exact timing of the transformation from the *polis* understood as fortified town, or even as the fortifications of the town, to the idea of the *polis* as a body of people is obscure.[2] The cause of the transformation is similarly obscure although it may well be that it developed as a consequence of sharing common adversity. The organised fighting manoeuvres of the Greek hoplite marked a departure from collective but individualised fighting, to treating battle as incorporating both individual heroism and co-ordinated and collective actions. The development of such co-ordinated manoeuvres depended significantly on the common placing of trust in others involved in the manoeuvre. It is conceivable that the discussion of common concerns and the notion of equality that led to politics as an activity were born of the mutual respect and trust arising from the organised approach to battle.

Political Beginnings

Whatever the precise nature of the transformation from a pre-political to a political Greece may have been by the sixth century BC there was a diversity of forms of government in Greece. The fluidity of form of government, combined with a reasonable stability in other areas of life, allowed not only experimentation but also discussion about government and its nature. The importance of this period for the foundation of citizenship concepts can scarcely be overstated. A civilisation may endure for a considerable time but without frequent and often radical changes of ruling form, or it may collapse simply because of radical changes of rule. The Greek townships with their agricultural base were able to survive through different types of rule. In consequence of this combination of survival and change, discussion about the best form of rule became commonplace. The language of politics was born, and with it the idea of the citizen as a member of a *polis*.

It was in Athens that the idea of the citizen was first fully expressed. An economic crisis gave rise to a substantial anti-aristocratic movement. Solon, Archon of Athens about 594 BC, in reconciling the new wealthy classes with the dominant landed class, gave Athens laws which embodied ideals of equality and citizenship. The laws of Solon, no longer extant[3] but much commented upon, mark the beginning of Athenian pre-eminence in political thought. In a significant way, his rule also marked the beginning of a rich and meaningful concept of citizenship.

Solon gave all citizens the right of appeal from the magistrates to popular courts. It is said by Aristotle[4] and by Plutarch[5] that Solon deliberately framed his laws in an unclear manner so that they had to be judged by the popular courts. The popular courts included the Thetes, the lowest of four citizen classes. In consequence of these measures devised by Solon all citizens obtained a share in the operation of their own affairs. This basic principle of sharing in the operation of common affairs, and the sense of belonging which such sharing can engender, still underlies richer views of citizenship.

The idea of the importance of sharing in the operation of one's own life has rarely been better expressed than by Pericles in a panegyric to those fallen in the Peloponnesian war. The constitution of Athens, we are told, is a model for others, it favours the many not the few and for that reason is called a democracy. The laws of Athens afford justice to all in their private differences, and 'advancement in public life falls to reputation for capacity, class considerations not being allowed to inter- fere with merit ... if a man is able to serve the state he is not hindered by the obscurity of his condition'. [6]

Two thousand years later, in 1428, the words of Pericles were echoed by Bruni, this time about the Florentine city-state. After referring to Solon, Bruni, who modelled a panegyric to the fatally wounded General Nanni Strozi on that of Pericles, used similar words to express similar sentiments – this time about the Florentine city-state:

> The constitution we use for the government of the republic is designed for the
> liberty and equality of indeed all the citizens ... Virtue and probity are required
> of the citizens by our city. Anyone who has these two qualities is thought to be
> sufficiently well born to govern the republic. [7]

Privilege and Exclusivity

Citizenship in Greece was not for everyone: it was the status and privilege of a few. Freedom, which was required for, indeed a part of, citizenship, was a concept based on economic freedom. Greek life distinguished, therefore, between citizens and non-citizens. Nevertheless citizenship was a status jealously guarded and a privilege taken seriously. To be a citizen was a way of being among others as *zoon politikon*, as political being. To be was to be among men. Not to be among men was not to Be as a human.

It is against this understanding of what it is to be human that we can understand some of the reasons Socrates had for taking the poison hemlock as a punishment for his crimes, rather than taking, as his friends urged him to, exile. For Socrates, to face a life outside the *polis*, as a non-citizen, would be to face the prospect of a life that was not fully human. We might compare this situation with the situation of stateless persons today. All persons have rights as humans; but human rights are, for the most part, citizen rights – rights found in, and lived in, recognised nation-states.

There are thought to be dangers in resting the idea of rights, and a notion of Being, on the idea of citizenship rights, or on citizenship. The death of Socrates looked at as the choice between death and a life as a non-citizen, a non-human exile, provides one example of the power of the notion of citizenship. There are contemporary arguments pointing up the dangers of resting too much on the notion of citizenship. In considering the US legal attitude to the notion of citizenship, Alexander Bickel[8] has argued that as citizenship can be granted, or not granted, so it can be removed and any rights accruing from citizenship would also be lost. The view of the US Supreme Court, expressed by Justice Black, was that 'in our country the people are sovereign and the Government cannot sever its relationship to the people by taking away their citizenship'. [9]

Bickel, in arguing against Black's view, points out that 'A relationship between government and the people that turns on citizenship can always be dissolved or denied.' [10] He goes on to conclude that 'Citizenship is at best a simple idea for a simple government.' [11] Bickel prefers, therefore, to ground rights in the notion of person rather than the notion of citizen. Historically, however, the notion of a person is much more recent than the notion of a citizen,[12] and culturally even more restricted than the notion of a citizen. Indeed there is ample evidence to show that the relation between the notion of the person and the notion of the citizen depends historically and practically on the notion of a citizen. This is not to deny, however, that there are now tensions between the notions of person, self, individual, citizen and human and citizen. There are such tensions and they do have significant consequences.

Two Types of Citizen

Parallel to the development of the *polis* in Greece and the development of the idea of active, participatory citizenship is the development of Roman concepts of citizenship. The first Romans were probably Etruscans who founded the village that was later to become the city of Rome, around 700 BC. By that time the southern parts of Italy and Sicily had been settled by the Greeks, a situation that was not to change until the defeat of Pyrrhus in 274 BC.

The early form of Roman government was monarchical, but the last monarch, Tarquin, was deposed in 509 BC. when Rome became a republic. The earliest form of government of the new republic vested power in two consuls. These consuls, whose power was supreme, if temporary, held power for one year, each having the power to veto the decisions of the other. The agreement of both was required for a change in the law. In addition there was an advisory council, a senate, whose members were drawn from the patricians, the fathers of the community, and two assemblies.

The type of government established institutionalised differences between patrician and plebeian classes. Both classes were citizens, yet were distinguished by community and religious status. They were not allowed to intermarry. Plebeians were barred from the performance of some of the religious rituals that were necessary to high office. In consequence they were effectively barred from full participation in the life of the republic and from social advancement.

The effect of incorporating the class distinction between patricians and plebeians into citizenship was to distinguish between two forms of citizenship: citizenship as incorporating both participation and status, and citizenship as incorporating merely status.[13] This distinction between active and passive citizenship concepts was quite alien to Greek thought, as were the sentiments that went with it. Cicero divided the trades and professions into the liberal and the vulgar. He condemned 'the odious occupation of the collector of customs and the usurer and the base and menial work of unskilled labourers, for the very wages the labourer receives are a badge of slavery ...'. Only those of the liberal professions could advance to high office, and even that capacity was not entirely learnt. In a passage far from the sentiments of Pericles or Bruni he says that those '..whom nature has endowed with the capacity for administering public affairs should put aside all hesitation, enter the race for public office, and take a hand in directing the government ...'.[14]

For the vast majority of people, however, citizenship was a status, carrying rights and some duties but excluding the right or duty to participate in the political life of the republic. The rapid expansion of the Roman Empire was based less on the use of force and more on granting the status of valuable Roman citizenship to the conquered peoples. The value of Roman citizenship is, perhaps, best known through the appeal of St Paul, a citizen of Tarsus and of Rome, to Caesar. Arrested and bound in Jerusalem, Paul told those who held him that he was born a citizen of Rome. 'Those about to examine him moved immediately away from him as did the Tribune who was afraid knowing fully that he had bound a Roman citizen.'[15]

To be a citizen of Rome was to have a valuable legal status. If challenged it provided protection. It allowed much free and unhindered movement across the empire and stimulated peaceful trade and, for some, a cosmopolitan outlook. It did not endow, however, an automatic right to participate in affairs of the republic. When St Paul visited Athens he met donnish attitudes. Athens was just one more minor city of the empire; 'the Athens of Pericles was to dwindle into the Athens of St. Paul'. [16]

Yet if the problem of Greece had been a failure to transcend the parochial, if participatory, concept of citizenship to produce a co-ordinated Hellenistic federation the problem of Rome was its very opposite. Granting, even encouraging, dual citizenship to the people of its empire was significant and important; it gave something to the people (which was not always a worthless abstraction, as we see with Paul's appeal to Caesar), rather than merely taking from a population, as in a barbarian pillage. Dual citizenship also placed a strain on loyalties which Rome was never entirely able to transcend.[17] This problem of divided loyalties bedevils contemporary attempts to form federations of larger groups. To be a citizen of England, Scotland, France, even perhaps a citizen of Serbia for example, and a citizen of Europe at the same time is a challenge yet to be fully met. Failure at this task would have echoes of the failure of Greece to federalise sovereign city-states. It would also have echoes of the failure of Rome to manage fully the problems of the divided loyalties of dual citizenship.

Status and the Inward Turn

If Greece was to be the source of a participatory idea of citizenship as a vital part of communal being, Rome gave to its citizens, wherever they might be, a vital legal and often dual status. The Greek ideal of the citizen was a mode of life: dual or multiple citizenship, and dual or multiple loyalties, formed no part of that notion. By contrast, except for Romans narrowly defined as citizens of the city of Rome, dual loyalty, to the city of birth and to the empire, if not the city of Rome, was normal and expected. The contrast is exemplified in the difference between Socrates, for whom life outside the city is a life stripped of humanity, and St Paul, for whom Roman citizenship had no significant bearing on his life's work additional to the utility of safety that it offered him.

It is into the contrast between citizen as being and citizen as status that a new and significant self-understanding was introduced. This is the Christianised notion of person, the notion that Alexander Bickel places weight upon in preference to the notion of the citizen. The notion of person itself has two distinct origins. The first, Greek, from *prosopon*, refers to a mask such as an actor would wear, as in the related Latin *personae dramatis*. The second notion of person, more Roman-legal, refers to a person as one having a certain kind of legal status, a legal identity.

To be a person in Roman law is not a status ascribed before birth, as a foetus, a position St Thomas Aquinas was to maintain in the thirteenth century. Nor was it a status automatically given at birth, as an automatic consequence of live birth. Personhood in Rome was accorded when the father raised, or lifted, the new-born child from the floor, thus accepting the new child into the community. If he failed to do this the child would be placed in the street as being of no significance.[18]

The Christian notion of person, by contrast with either the Greek or Roman concepts, shifted personhood into the domain of religion and metaphysics. By modelling the idea of human personhood on the person-hood of God the idea of the human person began to acquire a status that no legal notion of citizenship or personhood could, itself, complete. The injunction, 'render the things of Caesar to Caesar and the things of God to God',[19] is often taken to have drawn a distinct boundary between the life of the city and the life of the spirit.

More widely, and far more significantly, by giving to the notion of personhood a divine imagery a new category of Being on Earth was created. This added a new justification to an older practice of turning away from, or being indifferent to, the life of the city. In some cases there was a complete withdrawal from communal life. The life of the extreme ascetic involves not merely the rejection of the body, of matter; it is also the rejection of the city.[20] Radical asceticism does not sit well with the idea or practice of citizenship, but even non-ascetic modes of Christianity have often found difficulties with the notion.

Christianity holds the life of the spirit and the life of the body in tension. The anonymous writer of a letter to Diognetus claims that Christians are no threat to secular authorities, but he also makes it clear that, Christians 'pass their time upon the earth, but they have their citizenship in heaven'. This tension in Being in the world runs into the very nature of being human, for as the anonymous writer makes clear, 'The soul dwells in the body but it is not of the body, and Christians dwell in the world, but are not of the world.'[21] These dualisms, which distinguish spirit and body and self and world, equate the imperfect body with an imperfect world and place the metaphysical person in a place other than the world, in the inner life.

This inner life, absent in Greek and much Roman writing, emerged from, and within, the Judaic-Christian encounter with the Graeco-Roman city. The sense of struggle with the materiality of the world, with releasing, or fostering, the eternal spirit within, the struggle with the human passions and the physical demands of the body, lie at the heart of emerging introspection. Success and failure became inner, not outer, categories, and the exhibition of the struggle lies not in the heroic saga of deeds done, of lands conquered, of enemies vanquished, but in the confession of inner life.

No one represents this fundamental change in outlook more clearly than Augustine of Hippo, in whose *Confessions* the externalised saga of an earlier culture is turned to the inner narrative of a world yet to come. Augustine's writings exhibit both the emerging sense of self and the emerging understanding of free will as a concept that would link self and world. His early work, *On Free Choice of the Will*, confirms the Greek view of a good citizen making communal decisions on grounds of common interest.

His later work turns away from the world towards another kind of city. This retreat, this turning away from the world, was given additional impetus with the fall of Rome, sacked by Alaric in 410. In an influential argument, Augustine pointed out that Rome's many gods had failed to protect the city, which had become depraved in religious matters. The true route to salvation lay through Christ, whose coming had been prophesied in the scriptures. The love of worldly things and the turning away from God resulted in two cities: an earthly city that glorified itself, and a heavenly city that glorified God.

Augustine classified humans into two branches, one of which lives by human standards and the other that lives according to God's will. He then went on to argue, in a doctrine of incalculable influence, that the course of a person's life was known to God from eternity: 'by two cities I mean two societies of human beings, one . . . is predestined to reign with God for all eternity, the other doomed to undergo eternal punishment with the Devil.' [22] These two cities were created by different kinds of love, 'the earthly city . . . by self-love reaching the point of contempt for God, the Heavenly City by the love of God carried as far as contempt itself . . .'. [23] But in denying the world to affirm God, in denying the contemptible self, it is the self, paradoxically, that is affirmed.

To regard the self as contemptible is, nevertheless, to pay regard to the self. It is to raise that which had not hitherto been worthy of attention or comment, to something that was worthy of attention and comment. Augustine's contempt of the passionate worldly self confirms the inward turn. It was that inward turn which permitted, even encouraged, the interchange of citizenship and subjection; where the life of the citizen was surrendered in return for the life of a subject; where republics are exchanged for kingdoms.

Withdrawal and Return: Withdrawal

The monastic life, the life of withdrawal from the world, both preceded and followed the emergence of Christianity. It is part of, but is not unique to, Christianity. What is unique is the combination of circumstances that placed such a clear statement of the self and its torments at the end of the dominion of the city of Rome. As the city collapsed, so the self emerged; as the folly of the life of that city became clear, so a withdrawal into the life of the mind became attractive.[24]

The good once understood as civic virtues was now understood in predominantly internal terms: in terms of the self. More than a millennium after Augustine the full implications of that inward turn were expressed in the Kantian injunction to act on the moral law within. On this view it is from within the self that the standards appropriate to external action can be found.

For the forms of life emerging in the west following the fall of Rome that standard came to include following the dictates of lawfully established authorities; of being a lawful and law-abiding subject. For Pope Nicolas I (858–67) the implication of Augustine's doctrine of the two cities was not their separation but the dominance of secular power by papal power. This doctrine, while influential as an idea, was never to predominate completely in practice. As an idea, however, the view that the profane should be ultimately subordinate to the sacred was both powerful and persistent.

In the emerging world view humans occupied a place in the great chain of being, and the given places reflected the plan of God. Aquinas was able to write, without apparent contradiction, both that law was obtained by inward reflection, by reason; and that virtue consisted in following the law of another. For

> a law is nothing else than a dictate of reason in the ruler by which his subjects are governed. Now the virtue of any subordinate thing consists in its being well subordinated to that by which it is regulated.[25]

There is no contradiction for Aquinas, for it is the proper place of the ruler to use reason to give law and the proper place of the subject to use reason to obey the law of the ruler. Quoting Aristotle in support of his view he says, 'the virtue of every subject consists in his being well subjected to his ruler'. What he fails to say is that he has moved this quotation from its context in the life of the city and placed it with the life of the subject. It is the view of Aquinas that men are obliged to obey the ruler, but the bondage of such obedience is merely of the flesh and not of the soul.[26] Thus the argument for obedience, and subjection, to secular rulers is closed and complete: another loop in the medieval circle.

Nevertheless there is a small opening in this loop of subjection, an opening that came to be of some consequence for the modern world. There might be occasions when the reason of the ruler resulted in positive laws that violated the greater harmony. The ruler might require his subjects to act contrary to God's law. Such a law, a tyrannical law, Aquinas argues, would not be in accord with reason and therefore not a law. The lingering question in such a case is: who is to decide?

The mechanism for such a decision is that of conscience. Conscience is understood by Aquinas first, and traditionally, as *conscienta*, the judgment of the type of an action made by the actor and, second, as the view or judgment that an action ought or ought not to have been done.[27] That change of meaning, was pre-figured, but not fully developed, in the injunctions of Paul.[28] Fully developed it continues the inward turn.

The meaning and force of the concept of conscience was moved by Aquinas from an uncritical ground in external, shared, knowledge, to a critical inward ground.[29] The Augustinian view of freedom of will combined with this inner voice of conscience provided an opening both for disobedience and, later, for individual autonomy. The examination of proposed acts by the inner application of reason is, for Kant, the basis of both the Categorical Imperative and individual autonomy. In providing the grounds for obedience to secular authority Aquinas also provided the grounds for a challenge to that authority.

Withdrawal and Return: Return

There is no single source or aspect underlying the return to the life of the city. There were rather a variety of movements fed by different strains placed upon the great chain of being. The tensions between the church and the re-emerging life of the city, together with the embryonic idea of the modern state are, however, of considerable significance.[30]

The best known source of the republican revival is found in the emergence of, and pride in, city life in Italy. When Bruni praises Nanni Strozzi, he also praises Florence, its history, its traditions of freedom and civic virtue and its citizens, as Pericles before had praised Athens and its virtues. Even before Bruni's panegyric, both Dante and Marsilius of Padua had made significant statements of political theory that distinguished the role of the church from the role of the state. Marsilius, referring to Aristotle's *Politics*, defines a citizen 'as one who participates in the civil community', and is insistent that law-making properly 'belongs only to the whole body of the citizens or the weightier part thereof'.[31]

The sharp distinction drawn by Marsilius presages a wider move to distinguish the sacred and the profane with a new emphasis being placed upon the right form of government for the earthly city. The basis of that new form of government is found not merely in a revival of the city, but also in the development of a new concept; the concept of the state where that is understood as an abstract notion.

The differences between the Greek city and the modern state are many and significant. Not least is that the Greek *polis* was a form of life, and not merely a thing. Even the Latin *res-publica*, literally 'the public thing', denotes a shift from the community nature of the *polis* towards a less intimate form of political life. In Athens all citizens were able to participate in public life. In the empire of Rome all citizens shared a formal status, but only citizens of a certain class were able to participate in public life. The Greek *polis* is not then a city-state; it is a mode of life.

The modern state is an abstract and legal concept whose roots are to be found in the idea of autonomy within a certain territory. Even in some early thinking it was coupled to the view that the state belongs to no person in particular.[32] Such a view of the state is ultimately subversive to the idea of any particular personage having unfettered autonomy over the lives of the people. On this view, a view that took some time to be fully developed, a king, contra the claim of Louis XIV that 'L'etat et moi,' may be a symbol of the state, but is not the state.

What is evident at this time is the oscillation between, the tension between, the recurring idea of the citizen as actively sharing a life and the citizen as one sharing a status. The former idea, which appealed to an earlier Athens, recurred most fully in cities in Germany and in Italy. The latter idea, the citizen as a more or less passive bearer of rights, appealed more in the embryonic state. Bodin, rejecting the idea of the citizen as a participant in public affairs, tells us that 'It is a very grave error to suppose that no one is a citizen unless he is eligible for public office. . .' [33] A citizen is a free subject, but 'It is therefore the submission and obedience of a free subject to his prince, and the tuition, protection, and jurisdiction exercised by the prince over his subject that makes the citizen.' [34] The concern which Bodin exhibits is a concern for order; a concern echoed by Hobbes when faced with the consequences of a civil war.

The idea of participation in the shape of one's life is, however, a powerful one. Even before Hobbes' absolutist response to the events in England, Starkey produced an imaginary dialogue of considerable importance and influence. Starkey, influenced by the Italian civic humanists and by the thought of Aristotle, took the view that the function of political theory was to advise rulers. Philosophers should seek to educate and influence kings. It was intended that his imaginary dialogue between Pole and Lupset would be presented to Henry VIII. In the event it is unclear whether it was presented to the king; and publication did not happen in Starkey's lifetime.

The dialogue between Pole and Lupset is a form of word play in which quite radical positions and viewpoints are aired. At one point Starkey has Pole say 'For what is more repugnant to nature, than a whole nation to be governed by the will of one prince ... What is more contrary to reason.' [35] Not content with this, he contrasts the elected rulers of Greece with the idea of heredity rule: 'This succession of princes by inheritance and blood was brought in by tyrannous and barbarous princes, which as I said is contrary to nature and all right reason . . .'. [36] Being a mere subject it seems is contrary to nature and reason.

The emergence of the inner life forces a distinction between two separate senses of subjectivity. Being subject to another and being a subject for oneself are distinct but intertwined ideas. The distinction is present in the writing of Augustine, where it abetted the withdrawal from the city. At a later time it was to abet the return. Augustine's claim that, 'If I am mistaken, I exist', comes a millennium earlier than Descartes' *Cogito ergo sum*: 'I think, therefore I am.' Augustine included also the reflective, 'For just as I know that I exist, I also know that I know.' [37]

For both Augustine and Descartes the existence claim came from a withdrawal into the examination of the mind. But where an entire age followed Augustine into the *vita contemplativa* the age following Descartes found freedom in their subjectivity, in a newly discovered individualism. Hobbes, in a petulant, even angry, exchange with Bishop Bramshill, repeated an earlier claim that the actions of men were determined according to causal laws. In *Leviathan* he claimed that the idea of freedom of will was a contradiction, there was only freedom from opposition.[38]

What was at stake in this kind of disagreement was the emerging notion of autonomy, understood first as freedom of the self, free will, but also having political consequences. The idea is a simple one, if human beings have free will, if they are autonomous concerning themselves, then they are sovereign concerning their own actions. If they are sovereign in that respect, then there are no good grounds for surrendering to or being subject to another against their will.

Ultimately the inward turn, the withdrawal into the self away from the city, seems to have been a period in which the grounds for renewal and return were laid. The idea of sovereign individuals is so subversive of existing order that it is little wonder that Hobbes while celebrating individualism should also place it under the influence of scientific, causal laws. But for Rousseau, and for Kant, the very hallmark of the human individual is freedom of the will, autonomy rather than heteronomy. Human life fully led is the life of a moral self demanding virtue in action and justice in laws. In Kant's practical philosophy this does not lead to revolutionary proposals; on the contrary he makes it serve a modest conservatism.

Kant's underlying idea of the subject as the ground of experience was, however, metaphysical dynamite. In the Kantian notion of the transcendental subject, where subjectivity requires a ground of experience not itself caused by experience, the idea of the autonomous subject reached its apotheosis. The assumption of the transcendental subjectivity of the mind released the political subject from the last vestiges of the great chain of being and from the reasons of political subjection. As Kant celebrated the autonomous subject in his philosophy, so autonomous subjects, blissfully unaware of this revolution in thought, took matters into their own hands and replaced the French monarchy with the Republic of France.

Revolution and Beyond

The representatives of the people of France meeting as the newly established National Assembly declared that 'ignorance, neglect or contempt of certain rights are the sole causes of public misfortune'. In resolving to correct this, the assembly declared 'in the presence of the Supreme Being [to recognise the] ... *sacred* rights of men and of citizens'.[39]

The principal intention of the declaration was to give practical force to political change and to signal the new order. The form of words, however, is important for it places the rights of man and the rights of the citizen together as having sacred status. By holding the two concepts together in this way, both in the preamble to the declaration and throughout the declaration itself, it is made clear that the rights of the citizen are not separate from and additional to human rights.

The rights of and the right to be a citizen, to be and to have a share in the operation of one's own country, are not, on the principles of this declaration, distinct from human rights. By the principles attached to the declaration, citizenship, membership of the body politic, was accorded to all men born, and resident, in France. As citizenship incorporated membership of the body politic, so citizenship was active, participatory in principle and not merely an expression of passive rights, of mere status. In this respect the declaration looked to civic virtues, to the life of the city. It was not long, however, before the assembly began to move away from these ideals and look towards distinguishing participatory from non-participatory citizens.[40]

By October 1789, in a move reminiscent of an earlier Rome, citizens were divided into two types: those who could vote and those who could not, active citizens and passive citizens. In a scathing attack on this distinction Robespierre claimed that this 'new expression' was 'a cover for the most flagrant violation of the rights of man'.[41] Under the terms of the 1789 law the assembly decreed payment of a poll tax as a voting qualification. Deputies to the assembly were to be chosen by a body of electors. The electors, who had to pay a further tax, were chosen by those who had paid the basic poll tax.

Robespierre, in a speech to the assembly, the irony of which is not entirely lost even today, castigates the assembly concerning four propositions that mitigate against the citizenship values of the declaration. With 'No ... No ... No ... No ... All men *born* and *domiciled* in France are members of the body politic'. he dismisses the arguments for a poll tax.

For,

> what is the worth of my much vaunted right to belong to the sovereign body if
> the assessor of taxes has the power to deprive me of it ... and if it is subject at
> once to the caprice of man and the inconstancy of fortune?[42]

In the elections to the National Convention of September 1792 Robespierre's demands met with partial success. By 1794, however, Robespierre had lost the argument, his position and his head.

The French Revolution that had started with such idealistic promise degenerated into an admixture of hypocrisy and terror. The reaction to the French Revolution was far from universally favourable. Not only did the revolution demonstrate ideals that were anathema to many, but its actual practice verged between the farcical and the tragic. Writing before the full effects of the terror Edmund Burke mocked the elaborate and convoluted voting system that effectively denied force to the declaration.

Burke's complaint is not so much that the declaration is imperfectly instantiated, though he certainly mocks its practice, as that it is based on abstract and unrealisable theory. Burke does not want to deny 'the *real* rights of men',[43] but those rights are found not in abstract declarations but in real arrangements in society. Society is a contract between the living, the dead and those not yet born. A revolution breaches that contract in the name of abstract principles. 'Government is a contrivance of human wisdom to provide for human wants ... Society requires not only that the passions of individuals should be subjected, but ... their will controlled and brought into subjection.' [44] In asserting this, Burke turns away from the idea and ideal of autonomy back to the notions of lordship and subjection. Freedom for the French meant that 'these pretended citizens' [45] have behaved towards their own country as if it were a 'country of conquest'.[46]

Burke was undoubtedly correct that the people of France could not learn how to govern merely from abstract principles, but his own views on subjection of the will amounted to justifying the continuing conquest of his own country. Sometimes one might well, and reasonably, maintain that subjection should be thrown off; even if the future beyond the revolution is uncertain. Such was the view taken by the framers of the American Declaration of Independence, a full thirteen years before the revolution in France.

The bond that tied the peoples of the American colonies to another people was to be dissolved. That dissolution, it was held, was an act that the subject people were absolutely entitled to undertake. In a phrase containing a motif to recur in the Declaration of the Rights of Man and of the Citizen it was asserted that all men were created equal, 'and are endowed by their creator with certain unalienable rights'.[47] A form of government may become destructive of the ends for which it was

created; serving the people. In such case the people may dissolve the
ties with that government and resume their original power.[48] Such was
held to be the case with George III the king of England abusing his
position concerning the thirteen colonies. In such a case it is the right
of the people, perhaps even their duty, to rescind that form of government and exchange it for another.

The idea that a government can be removed if it is tyrannical or
acting against natural or divine law is scarcely new. The tyrants of
ancient Greece were forcibly removed. More recently, in that age of
transition when a few western thinkers rediscovered and re-examined
Aristotle, Aquinas had provided limits to sovereign secular authority.
With those limits he had also provided a theological basis for resistance
in extremis. The ideas of Aquinas had found their way into English
political thought in the writings of Hooker.[49] The 'Judicious Hooker' is
referred to by Locke in a text that finds in the natural law tradition
both justification for government and the grounds for dissolving that
government.[50]

In dissolving the colonial ties with the king of England, the Declaration
of Independence makes it clear the laws of nature are held, in accordance
with tradition, to be prior to positive law. But where Aquinas took natural
law to be supportive of the inequalities of positive law the declaration
takes it, with Locke, that inequality is found only in positive law. Thus the
claim that 'We hold these truths to be self evident, that all men are created
equal . . .' is anything but self-evident. On the contrary it was a claim that
emerged slowly, more than a millennium after the city had been abandoned, and when it did emerge it emerged imperfectly, for the term 'men'
excluded women and slaves.

The 1789 Declaration of the Rights of Man and of Citizens fell to
the hubris of the terror. The increased stability of the United States did
not, however, prevent the Declaration of Independence and the Constitution of the United States falling to its own particular kind of hubris.
Matters of citizenship were matters of law and of jurisprudence. What
counts as a person, what counts as a citizen, what counts as a man are,
for the United States, then as now, constitutional questions to be
settled by recourse to law.

When faced in 1857 with the question of whether a Negro could sue
in the court of Missouri, the Supreme Court ruled that he could not,
that the district court of Missouri had no jurisdiction.[51] The fine words
of the Declaration of Independence, it was held, did not apply to 'the
Negro race', who were regarded by the Constitution 'as a separate class
of persons'. The court held that the words '"people of the United
States" and "citizens" are synonymous terms, and mean the same thing'.
Every citizen is a part of the sovereign people and the class of persons

who are Negro are not 'included and not intended to be included, under the word "citizens"'.[52] It follows from this judgment that two classes of person were constructed by the court: persons able to exercise all the rights and privileges in the union and persons unable to exercise such rights and privileges.[53] Citizenship rights are necessary to the exercise of full personhood.

This same point was made at a different time and a different place by Anna Barbauld. Anna Barbauld was active in the English dissenters movement at the end of the eighteenth century. Inspired by the French ideal, the movement sought to widen the parliamentary franchise. Barbauld mocks the view that such claims should take the form of a request: 'As we were suppliants, we should have behaved like suppliants, and then perhaps – No, Gentlemen, we wish to have it understood, that we do claim it as a right. It loses otherwise half its value.' [54] The force of her argument is that to lack citizen rights is to be excluded from civil office, from position, place and influence. The form of opposition generated is a function of the opposition met. In an almost Foucaultian polemic she makes it clear that the party of dissenters is a construct, a creation, a function of opposition.[55] If the dissenters seem alien, that is because 'It is you, who by considering us as Aliens, make us so.' [56]

Again and again it emerges with some clarity that it is not because people are equal that they are granted citizen rights; it is because people demand and obtain citizen rights that they become equal persons. The same point was made, albeit in a different way, by other groups exhibiting dissent. The London Corresponding Society, a group inspired by and established in reaction to the French Revolution, persisted with the theme of reconstructing the very notion of man. They showed a concern with, and an awareness of, the relation between being a citizen and being human. 'Man as an individual is entitled to liberty, it is his Birth-right', [57] they asserted.

The clear implication of the claim of the London Correspondents is that a human without liberty is not a human, is deprived of something crucial. But it is not mere liberty, a mere letting go, that is required: it is citizenship. They grant that some rights are given up in the process of being in association with others, in society. It is a clear consequence of this that unless one has the 'right of sharing in the government of his country ... no man can, with truth call himself free'. [58]

What is emerging in these strands of thought is the slow, but definite, recognition that terms such as 'man/woman/Negro' and their cognates denote little more than biological features and of themselves carry little moral weight. The term 'human' has both a biological and a moral connotation, but in social and philosophical matters the moral dimension to being human is not a mere consequence of human biology. Being a moral being is an ineliminable part of one's humanity. And moral equality requires equality in the body politic.

If we are not free then it is not that we are degraded; it is that we are, in some significant way, not human. Rousseau made just this claim when he argued that to surrender one's liberty was to surrender one's humanity.[59] It was this position, if imperfectly expressed, coupled with a sense that the key to freedom lies in sharing in government, that is to be found emerging in the minutes of the London Corresponding Society. What is emerging, or more accurately re-emerging after two millennia or more, in the wilderness, is a sense that to be human is to be a citizen.

A continent and half a century away from these voices of dissent Lincoln was facing the same issues. 'Four score and seven years ago', he said at Gettysburg in 1863, and just five years after the *Dred Scott* case, a new nation had been created, 'conceived in Liberty and dedicated to the proposition that all men are created equal'. The civil war was testing that nation's endurance, but it was his resolve that 'this nation under God shall have a new birth of freedom'.

Lincoln reminded his audience that the United States was based on the proposition that all men were created equal. In saying this he was well aware that what counted as a man had, for seventy years, been determined by who and what counted as a citizen. His plea, therefore, that 'this nation, under God, shall have a new birth of freedom – and that government of the people, by the people, for the people, shall not perish from the earth',[60] was fraught with difficulty. In the language of *Dred Scott*, 'citizen' and 'people' were interchangeable terms, so the full realisation of this claim meant nothing less than the reconstitution of the people. It also meant nothing less than the reconstitution of the citizenry; of the city as symbol. That is a task which no laws and no wars can, by themselves, meet.

The Reconstitution of the City as Symbol

The turn away from the city represented an unsuccessful experiment with a life outside human company. For a millennium an entire civilisation had turned away from the life of the city. The return to the city as mode of life and as symbol was no mere turning back to a past age. It involved, rather, a reconstruction of the very idea of what it was to be human and of what it was to be involved in human life. The new constituents of the city were separated from the great chain of being, and from the feudal order. They existed not as members of a community but as individuals living beside other individuals.

To come to communal life, to living among rather than beside one another, required, and still does require, the construction of new forms of understanding. The view that the notion of the citizen can serve this purpose is not without its difficulties, and not without its critics. The most challenging kind of criticism is that the very idea of the citizen is abstract, based on particular interests and, even if fully realised, falls short of meeting human needs. This is the effect of the claim made by Marx in one of his early essays.

The 'Essay on the Jewish Question' challenges some of the fundamental categories and distinctions which people bring to bear on their being and within which they live their lives. Marx develops a full-blown critique of the idea of political emancipation and of the idea of citizenship. The categories within which people perceive themselves and are perceived, such as Jew or German or citizen, fall short of, and may even mitigate against, human emancipation. To achieve emancipation as a Jew, for example, is to confirm the distinction between Jewishness and the Christian state. It is to seek a privilege, to go cap in hand – as Anna Barbauld earlier had refused to do.

To seek and to obtain citizenship as a Jew, a German or, we might add now as relevant examples, a woman, a black or other distinction, is to seek, and possibly obtain, political emancipation. Political emancipation in confirming the original distinction can be at best, but a stage in the process of obtaining full human emancipation. Political emancipation is progressive, for it is the final form of emancipation within the social order of the times. For all that it is reductive, separating man into the components of individual and citizen; 'it is reduction of man, on the one side to the member of bourgeois society, to the egoistic, independent individual, and on the other side, to the citizen, to the moral person'. [61] True human emancipation is not a reduction but a restoration of man who incorporates into his being the abstract citizen and his individuality. When this has occurred then he will recognise and arrange his own life so that social and political power will not be distinguished; then 'human emancipation will be achieved'. [62]

Marx's criticism of political emancipation is profound and telling. His claim that citizenship is but a partial mode of being and only a partial solution to the ills of the time, points up an issue that is only now being addressed; that one of the greatest challenges to order and mutual respect in contemporary western societies is an excessive reliance on exclusive partial identities. Where Marx is wrong, however, is in his claim that citizenship is merely an abstract device that substitutes for human emancipation. It may become such a device; at certain times, not excluding the present, it has undoubtedly taken on excessively juridical qualities. It may even be, more or less deliberately and cynically, utilised as an anti-emancipatory device. What is wrong with Marx's view is not the claim that the 'citizen' was being treated as an abstract, juridical, moral, entity separated from 'Man'. It is his view that human emancipation, being fully human, is a condition distinct from the condition of being a full citizen, having a share in the operation of one's own life.

It seems to be the case that the tradition of understanding oneself as being human, which in Marx's early writing means being conscious of one's self as a member of a species, cannot be separated from the tradition of some participatory concept of citizenship. The question for modern life in the early part of this century was whether that rich, participatory concept of citizenship was to be obtained within the form of the state; or by some other means. It is from the perspective of treating the state as institution and idea, as an idea with unfolding practical potential, that Muirhead, representing the distinctive strand of English Idealism, said, 'To deny one's citizenship is to deny one's humanity.'[63]

English Idealism takes the moral potential of the state seriously. For the members of society the state is 'the society of societies, the society in which all their claims against each other are mutually adjusted'.[64] From Green's perspective the state ideally realised has an absolute claim on the obedience of the citizens. The state, however, is never fully realised; it is always in a condition of imperfection. In consequence obedience is not unlimited, and where some sectional interest prevents the state attaining the public interest there may be a right to disobey. Correlatively there may be a duty to aid the state in advancing towards its ideal.

The reforming implications of the arguments of the idealists are clear and their impact was indeed in the area of reform and change. English Idealists attended to the state, for that was the form of the institution through which they saw modern life being expressed. The other side of the modern state, however, was the citizen. Where Marx had seen the citizen as abstract and juridical, Green saw citizenship as being based upon mutual recognition and association. In an argument evocative of Hegel's master–slave dialectic, Green suggests that the demands of mutual recognition render a right to treat one who is a slave in law as 'a man and a brother'. [65] The factor of social recognition is required before power is transferred into right. The clear implication of this line of argument is that the mere application of state power over a subject renders no right in that power. Legitimate state power depends on, among other things, mutual recognition by the members of society. This can be achieved through citizenship, but not through subjection.

Green's argument, and the related idealist writings, provided a significant theoretical underpinning for an important strand of reform. The state was a moral agent with duties towards its members. The interests of its members were served by mutual recognition and that was best achieved through democratic citizenship. Such a form of being together was untried, but for Henry Jones of world significance. Democracy, if successful, could 'show the world the way to a very great and growing good'.[66] Jones made it clear that he thought citizenship at the very heart of democracy and well being. 'The experiment ... of Democracy', he argues, 'will prosper in the degree in which it knows true citizenship; and it will know the truth in the degree in which it seeks it.' [67] For Jones the state has a moral capacity and its 'service, in consequence is the way of the better life for its citizens'. [68] This better life is not merely having the right to vote, extending the franchise, for if that were the limit to citizenship then it would be 'but an empty inheritance'.[69]

The recovery of the inheritance of citizenship lies in the recognition that being is also political being, of the mutual recognition of equals participating in a shared life and sharing in the operation of their own life. The initial growth of the state, which coincided with the emergence of the modern individual, mitigated against personal autonomy. Its concern was with security internal and external. The excessive Hobbesist concerns with security, however, are not the concerns of a settled society, and 'it is fullness of life and not merely immunity from aggression, which is the test of real freedom. The real freeman is the developed man.' [70] The sentiments expressed here would not be contentious to those inclined towards reform. The challenge is in achieving these aims in the conditions of mass society; as Laski put it, 'The scale of modern civilisation has of itself done much to deprive the citizen of his freedom.'[71]

In an argument that precedes some contemporary communitarian and pluralist views of citizenship, Laski points out that the solitary citizen would be unfulfilled. Citizenship on this account is not merely passive as status; it is also active. Citizenship is to be with others having a 'share in the disposal of [the] business' of the modern State '.[72] In practice few can participate in public office and citizenship has lost the spiritual energy with which it began life in Athens. Citizenship has become shaped by economic inequality and the very wants of the citizen of low economic status are shaped by others. In a statement relevant to some current thinking on citizenship, [73] Laski points out that consumption is an 'acceptance of enforced alternatives'. [74] The effect of this is a life in which there is no civic context. It is also a life in which 'citizens' are treated as objects of utility, as not being engaged in self-realisation. If humans are not engaged in self-realisation, if they are a means to an end rather than ends in themselves, then they are slaves, not true citizens.

Laski's conclusions about the human predicament are somewhat pessimistic. He could scarcely have agreed with Mandeville's rhyme in *The Fable of the Bees*,

> Thus every part was full of Vice,
> Yet the whole mass a Paradice ...
> And Vertue, who from Politicks

Had learn'd a Thousand cunning Tricks;
Was, by their happy Influence,
Made Friends with Vice: And ever since
The worst of all the Multitude
Did something for the common Good. [75]

For Laski a world that regards profit and competition as a source of
wellbeing is a world inimical to the project of citizenship. That project is
nothing less than self-realisation. The solution to the ills brought on by the
trap of consumption is the formation of co-operative groups to modify
consumption patterns. The co-operative movement has a power almost
without limit and needs to realise its political mission. He regards this as a
matter of some urgency for, 'Not since the fall of the Roman Empire has
the principle of Western Civilisation been in graver danger than in our own
day.' [76]

Just over half a century later Alasdair MacIntyre came to regard the
battle as lost. 'The new dark ages', he said, 'are already upon us ... This
time the barbarians are not waiting beyond the frontiers; they have already
been governing us for quite some time.'[77] What is at issue for MacIntyre is
whether new standards of community and civility can be forged in the
wake of the centrifugal force of individualism that has fragmented society.
What was at issue for Laski was a not entirely dissimilar thought.

The citizen as consumer is a citizen divorced from a concern for
general wellbeing, having a regard merely for the rights and activities of
consumption and not for the duties appropriate to being a citizen. His plea
in favour of co-operatives is partly a plea for the application of consumer
power to modify enforced consumer choices. It is also a communitarian
response to the potential problems of an excessively individualistic society.
That individualism has its roots in the transition from feudal to capitalist
society.

The change in the form of social relations which occurred with that
transition was a change from ascribed status to contract relations that
brought with it, at least the potential of, some bargaining power in
economic exchange relations. What it also brought with it was exploitation
and class relations. A problem generated by this change is that the very
recovery of citizenship, the project of citizenship, took place in a social
setting inimical to that project.

Citizenship contains within it the idea of equality, but class is
inherently unequal. Marx's solution to this problem had been to regard
citizenship as an abstraction, a juridical construct. Another reforming
perspective, however, might take citizenship as containing the potential
to undercut class inequalities, or to change them radically. The sociolo-
gist T.H. Marshall addressed just this question in an influential lecture
given at Cambridge in 1949. Marshall divided citizenship into three
different aspects: civil, including the right to freedom of movement and

the liberty to make contracts; political, including the right to be elected to public office or to be an elector; social, including the right to welfare provision and to share in the heritage of society.

This last aspect to citizenship, according to Marshall, can both break down traditional class barriers and produce newly legitimised stratifications. A central part of social rights is the right to education. Indeed education of oneself is a public duty as well as a personal right, for 'the social health of a society depends upon the civilisation of its members'.[78] In saying this Marshall is picking up a recurring theme in the modern revival of citizenship. In 1860 Mazzini had made a similar kind of exhortation: to make oneself and others more virtuous was not merely a right, it was a duty – the duty of a whole life. To achieve this required education, time and opportunity, for such education was not available in the context of a life of excessive labour. Without rights of citizenship, of participation in the actions which govern life, there can be no affection for the laws of the state.[79]

Marshall's argument is that the rights incorporated in the notion of citizenship developed at historically different times. The change from feudalism to capitalism exhibited, first, liberty rights, followed by political rights, and finally social rights as part of a progressive development. The notion of equality is central to the idea of citizenship. The role of education is central, for education makes equality of opportunity 'in this process of selection and mobility' [80] available as a right to citizens. The effect of this is to weaken hereditary privilege and to break the ties with the original class structure. However, education is tied to occupation, so the demands of 'citizenship operates as an instrument of social stratification'.[81] Citizenship replaces one form of stratification with another, legitimated on a different basis. Classes do not entirely disappear but they become more transitory and instrumental associations. Marshall argues that 'This might be described as a weakening of class in the Marxian sense, on the grounds that the operative interest groups are no longer determined by ... property.' [82]

An implication of Marshall's argument, if correct, is that in distinguishing between man and the abstract juridical citizen Marx failed to see the power of the idea of citizenship. Marx does claim that citizenship, as political emancipation, is worth seeking, but for all that political emancipation falls short of human emancipation. Marshall's distinction between the civil, political and social components of citizenship corresponds roughly to a distinction sometimes now drawn between first-, second- and third-generation rights. First-generation rights are rights of liberty, second-generation rights are rights of equality, and third-generation rights are rights of solidarity or fraternity. On this distinction the slogan of the French Revolution, Liberté, Egalité, Fraternité, represents a project with solidarity rights as the basis for the end stage: fraternity. Marshall's third stage of citizenship, social rights, is expressed as welfare provisions.

The issues from Marx's viewpoint would be, first, whether the achievement of social rights represents human emancipation and, second, whether citizenship has undercut class. A different sort of issue is whether Marshall's analysis assists in understanding the processes within newly emerging or newly redefined nation-states. Marshall intended his remarks to apply principally to Britain and makes no general historical claims.

Nevertheless the ideas of liberty, equality and fraternity are at least European-wide and do have partial expression in international declarations of human rights. More particularly it does seem to have been the experience of eastern Europe and the former Soviet Union that political changes were preceded by an unprecedented upsurge of activity in civil association. It is as if the political forms acted as fetters on the civil associations. This was successful only up to a point, after which, to paraphrase Marx, an epoch of social revolution began. That social revolution included, among other things, the demand for political equality; the legal recognition of the right to form civil associations; to move freely around; to leave and re-enter the country, and to exhibit minimal aspects of the status of citizenship. The cost, almost paradoxically, was some weakening of social and welfare rights. But these rights had been state-imposed and excluded civil and political rights.

Historically it does seem to have been the case that the revival and reconstruction of some concept of citizenship in western Europe was, at least partly, predicated on the freedom of movement that arose at the dawn of civil society. That freedom of movement in turn produced the principle of contractual relations and juridical equality. Juridical equality is but a short step from political equality. Marx does take it that all the political possibilities in the existing form of life have to be exhausted before that form of life will be totally transformed. We would expect, therefore, the narrative of political emancipation, and with it citizenship, to be fully written and developed before it is transcended.

However, citizenship contains within it the potential for pushing what passes for political emancipation towards social emancipation; even, perhaps, towards human emancipation. The problem with Marx's analysis of political emancipation is that he does not see the full possibilities within that idea. He does not see that political emancipation may produce sufficient social dissonance to generate a demand for emancipation in more than a merely political, juridical and abstract respect. Nor does he see that political emancipation can itself provide a foundation for rich and diverse civil associations that may cut across his analysis of class. This particular limitation in Marx's thought is a direct consequence of his turn from Hegel, of denying, or limiting, the long-term effects of ideas on life and life structures.

By contrast Marshall sees that juridical equality has led to political equality and to a demand for social rights, but he does not see the truly radical and transforming potential of the idea of social rights, as fraternity. He does see that new forms of social inequality with new legitimations could arise, but he does not see that the form of the new legitimation of new forms of inequality would itself be politically induced, and sustained, by a thin concept of citizenship.

Marshall understands citizenship predominantly as status, as having rights and claims against the state and against others. It does involve duties, but these are almost formal and are derived from the need to maintain rights and entitlements. Marshall's theory of citizenship is useful and dynamic. It charts the path of a particular kind of political and social development where the end is the achievement of a set of status rights and their associated duties. A fuller, richer, participatory concept of citizenship is embryonic, but underdeveloped, in his work. Marshall's citizen is a wanderer returning from the desert in search of respite and sustenance rather than someone looking to make a life in, to participate in and find modes of Being in, the city.

To this extent his analysis reflects the history of major post-feudal changes. It also has application to societies that are throwing off the shackles of authoritarianism; returning to the world after their own withdrawal. In concentrating on the latter aspects of western history, however, he limits his vision. The post-feudal citizen is primarily a subject with some added status. Concepts of citizenship developed from the feudal breakdown, from the emergence of what Marx called egoistic individuals, tend to be limited in some important respects, the most important of which centres on the possible transformation of the idea of citizenship.

The radical idea of citizenship involves no more and no less than its recovery and renewal. It is said that the priests of Nemi would put the divine Kings of the Wood to death rather than see them die of old age. Their spirit would then return anew, bringing with it the fresh vigour of new vegetation in the spring.[83] And so it is with the life of the city, put to death by Augustine, now ready to return with fresh vigour in the spring of self-hood.

Citizenship as a Project

Hitherto, there have been a thousand goals, for there have been a thousand peoples. Only fetters are still lacking for these thousand necks, the one goal is still lacking. Yet tell me brothers: if a goal for humanity is still lacking, is there not still lacking humanity itself. The goal for humanity is humanity itself.[84]

The history of past subjections and the analysis of continuing subjections show that human autonomy has been built on the back of group emancipation. Both are late in coming, both emerge in struggle and neither are granted; they are rightly demanded and rightly taken. The history of Being human shows that the idea of being a member of a species is late in coming, is culturally specific in its origins and even now is far from universally adopted. Tribal consciousness is still widely evident in the developed world.

The history of human Being shows that the idea of Being human develops in the wake of participatory ideas of citizenship. Neither in history nor in anthropology does one find peoples with a sense of being human who then come to develop the idea of citizenship. It is rather that the consciousness of exclusivity and superiority, *Hellenes* and *Barbaros*, Greeks and others, leads to the concept of the citizen, to the equal. It is the idea of equality applied to the most universal category, the species, which made the concept of the human possible.

Being human as an idea depends not upon biological similarity but upon enlarging the notion of being equal to the point where biological similarity comes to have a moral force. This equality depends, in turn, upon regarding oneself, and being regarded by others, as equal in common affairs, of having a share in the operation of one's life – of being a citizen. Marx pointed up the value of human emancipation but thought citizenship a merely abstract category. Marshall regarded citizenship as a dynamic concept but did not see its full potential for human emancipation.

It seems that political emancipation is not merely an abstract category on the way to human emancipation. Political emancipation, in the sense of being a full citizen, is an ineliminable part of human emancipation; it is yet to be achieved. Political emancipation, citizenship, is not dispensable in favour of some other form of emancipation. Personal autonomy is possible in the wake of group emancipation and being human is possible in the wake of being a citizen. When Marx talks about the rights of citizens and the rights of man as distinct and abstract notions, he draws the wrong inference. There is no citizen apart from the man, he says, and this is correct, but not for the reasons he suggests. It is rather that to be a man, to be a woman, to be a person, to be a self, to have a rich life of the mind, is also to be engaged in the *vita activa*, to be a citizen. If that is absent the rest will not be fully present.

What this suggests is that the stakes are high. Whoever determines the nature of the concept of the citizen determines the political, and human, shape of society. If citizenship is contained as status, to which some entitlements are attached, that status will effectively be that of the enfranchised subject; if that be freedom then, as Rousseau suggested, it will be a facade. Freedom, participation, sharing in the operation of one's life, having some degree of autonomy, are essential to the sense that one has a life of one's own. The opposite is an unwilling or even unwitting subservience or servility. Once equality in one sense is attained relative deprivation, beyond a certain point, becomes anomalous and the desire for equality in other senses can become critical.

Citizenship concepts, if rich enough, have emancipatory potential and can be used to demand, and to justify, a rise in the standards of human life and in the very sense of what it is to be human. What starts out as a notion of belonging, on the one hand, and exclusivity, on the other hand, enlarges to encompass the very idea of being human as being a species being. The idea of citizenship has deeply subversive and radical potential. For that reason it is in the interests of some in society to play it down, to side-track it, to limit it to a status or entitlement notion, even to turn it into the idea of the citizen as a consumer with a consumers' charter. Perhaps a great hubris of our time is that the concept of citizenship born of saga and of noble heroes, attached to and central to the age of virtue, struggled over with such passion and held to be of such value should enter the next millennium as a device through which consumers can register minor complaints.

The principle enunciated by and put into practice by Solon, that all citizens, whatever their class, participate in or at least share in the operation of their own affairs, underlies the idea of active citizenship. When such sharing is not a part of citizenship it is unlikely that the concept will serve more than minimal consumer requirements. What is additionally at issue in distinguishing between citizenship as status, and citizenship as participation, is the very shape of society itself. A participatory notion of citizenship cannot work merely within the confines of an atomised, and individualised, mass society. Such a notion works best within the confines of community, at subsidiary levels. It requires, therefore, meaningful devolution. At a less subsidiary level such a notion is compatible with, and finds comfortable, the growth of new political movements. More radically still, a rich concept of citizenship requires meaningful and significant activity which, in being unconfined to parliamentary arrangements, moves the domain of, and the activity of, the political into new areas.

What is at stake in current concerns about citizenship is nothing less than the task of rethinking the political, of rethinking and enlarging the concept of what it is to be human. Human beings describe themselves and understand themselves in numerous ways; as women, men, persons, selves, individuals and even citizens. What is clear from the history of citizenship and the history of Being human is that citizenship is not an optional extra, a mere add on, to what it is to be human. It is not that there are humans who have become citizens, it is rather that there are citizens with the capacity to grow into humanity.

Notes

1. James B. Pritchard (ed.) *Ancient Near Eastern Texts*, 3rd edn (Princeton, NJ: Princeton University Press, 1969), pp. 7–8.

2. Victor Ehrenberg, 'When Did the Polis Rise?' *Journal of Hellenic Studies* vol. LVII (1957), pp. 147–59, gives 800 BC. This is earlier than most commentators.

3. Fragments of Solon's poetry, some of which recount his political view, do survive. They were probably written after the end of his Archonship in 594 BC and before his death in 560 BC.

4. Aristotle, 'The Constitution of Solon' in *The Athenian Constitution* [329–325 BC], part 1, ch. 2, in John Warrington (ed.), *Aristotle's Politics and Athenian Constitution* (London: Dent, 1959), pp. 249–56.

5. *Plutarch's Lives*, vol. 1, tr. Bernadotte Perrin (Cambridge, Mass.: Harvard University Press, 1914), pp. 447–55.

6. Thucydides, *History of the Peloponnesian War*, [431 BC] Tr. Richard Crawley (London: Dent, 1912); see pp. 41 below.

7. L. Bruni, 'Oration for the Funeral of Nanni Strozi', in *The Humanism of Leonardo Bruni: Selected Texts*, New York Renaissance Society of America. (New York: State University of New York at Binghamton, 1987); see pp. 78 below.

8. Alexander M. Bickel, 'Citizen or Person? What is not Granted Cannot be Taken Away', in A. Bickel, *The Morality of Consent* (London: Yale University Press, 1975); see pp. 180–2 below.

9. Ibid. p.181.

10. Ibid. p. 182.

11. Ibid.

12. On the origins of the notion of a person see Marcel Mauss, 'A Category of the Human Mind: the Notion of Person; the Notion of Self' tr. Ben Brewster in Marcel Mauss, *Sociology and Psychology*, (London: Routledge and Kegan Paul, 1979).

13. A distinction that is hard to eliminate.

14. Cicero 'On Moral Duties', in *The Basic Works of Cicero* M. Hadras (ed.), tr. G.B. Gardiner, book 1 (New York: Random House, 1951) pp. 13-15.

15. Acts XXII, 29.

16. The phrase is from D.C. Somerville's edition of Arnold Toynbee's *A Study of History* (London: Oxford University Press, 1970), p. 927.

17. Ibid., ch. XVI.

18. W.V. Harris, 'The Roman Father's Power Over Life and Death', in R.S. Bagnall and W.V. Harris (eds), *Studies in Roman Law in Memory of A. Arthur Schiller* (Leiden: Brill, 1986), pp. 81–95. For recent and contemporary examples of similar social practices with respect to the newborn, see Helga Kuhse and Peter Singer, *Should the Baby Live?* (Oxford: Oxford University Press, 1985).

19. Luke XX, 25.

20. See Peter Brown, *The Body and Society: Men, Women and Sexual Renunciation in Early Christianity* (London: Faber and Faber, 1989).

21. Anon, 'The Epistle to Diognetus' [2nd–3rd century AD], *The Apostolic Fathers*, tr. Kirsopp Lake, (Cambridge, Mass.: Harvard University Press, 1913), vol. II., p. 61 below.

22. Augustine 'Concerning the City of God against the Pagans' [AD 413–16], book XV,(Harmondsworth:Penguin, 1972) p. 595.

23. Ibid., XIV, book 28 p. 593.

24. Arendt treats this as the inversion in the tradition between the life of action, *vita activa*, and the life of contemplation, *vita contemplativa*. The change is well captured in this distinction, what is less well emphasised is the tormented inwardness within the *vita activa* and the implication of this for the emergence of the self and subjectivity. Hannah Arendt, *The Human Condition* (Chicago: Chicago University Press, 1958). See also Charles Taylor, *Sources of the Self: The Making of Modern Identity* (Cambridge: Cambridge University Press, 1989).

25. *Summa Theologica* [1266–73], I-II qu. 92 article 1; see p. 64 below.

26. Ibid.,II–II qu. 104 article 6.

27. Ibid., I.a qu. 69 article 13.

28. E.g. 1 Corinthians VIII, 5; Romans VIII, 10; 2 Corinthians IV, 2.

29. C.S. Lewis, *Studies in Words* [1959] (Cambridge: Canto, 1990) ch. 8; see below pp. 191–6.

30. The role of the guild in fostering the autonomous city in early medieval Germany is traced in Antony Black, *Guilds and Civil Society in European Political Thought from the Twelfth Century to the Present*, (London: Methuen, 1984).

31. Marsilius of Padua, *Defensor Pacis* [1324], tr. A. Gewirth, Mediaeval Academy Reprints for Teaching, vol. 6. (Toronto: Toronto University Press, 1980) see p. 70 below.

32. The emergence of the concept of the state is dealt with most fully in Quentin Skinner, *The Foundations of Modern Political Thought* (Cambridge: Cambridge University Press, 1978), 2 vols.

33. Jean Bodin, *Six Books of the Commonwealth* [1576], ed. M.J. Tooley (Oxford: Blackwell, 1955), see p. 87 below.

34. Ibid. pp. 88–9.

35. Thomas Starkey, 'A Dialogue Between Pole and Lupset' [1535], ed. J.M. Cowper *England in the Reign of King Henry the Eighth*. part II: *A Dialogue Between Cardinal Pole and Thomas Lupset by T. Starkey* (London: Early English Text Society, 1878) see p. 86 below.

36. Ibid.

37. Augustine, *City of God*, book XI, ch. 26, p. 466.

38. Thomas Hobbes, 'Leviathan', ch. 5 in C.B. MacPherson (ed.) *Leviathan* (Harmondsworth:Penguin, 1968) p. 113.

39. Preamble to the 'Declaration of the Rights of Man and of Citizens by the National Assembly of France' [1789] in Thomas Paine *The Rights of Man*, ed. Hypatia B. Bonner (London: Watts and Co, 1937); see p. 115 below.

40. An idea also found in Kant's writing. It seems that Kant did not himself completely see the radical practical effects of his theoretical writing.

41. Maximilien Robespierre 'On the Right to Vote' in George Rudé, (ed.), *Robespierre* (Englewood Cliffs, NJ: Prentice-Hall, 1967); see p. 119 below.

42. Ibid. pp. 119 and 121.

43. Edmund Burke, *Reflections on the Revolution in France* (Harmondsworth: Penguin, 1973), p. 149.

44. Ibid. p. 151.

45. Ibid. p. 297.

46. Ibid. p. 298.

47. 'Declaration of Independence', 1776; see p. 111 below.

48. The relation between this view and the position maintained by John Locke in *The Second Treatise of Government* is notable. See Locke, *The Second Treatise of Government: an Essay Concerning the True Original, Extent and End of Civil Government* [17XX], ed. Peter Laslett (New York: New American Library, 1963).

49. Richard Hooker, *The Laws of Ecclesiastical Polity* [16XX]. eds A.S. McGrade and Brian Vickers (London: Sidgwick and Jackson, 1975).

50. Locke, *The Second Treatise of Government*. The reference to Hooker is in Section 5.

51. Dred Scott *v*. Sandford 1857.

52. Dred Scott *v*. Sandford 1857. Chief Justice Roger B. Taney for the Supreme Court.

53. James Madison had argued in 1787 that the constitution held slaves as part property and part persons. Insofar as they were persons they had the basic legal protection of life, insofar as they were property they were not entitled to representation, to a share in government. James Madison, 'The Federalist Papers' extracted in P.A.B. Clarke and A. Linzey, (eds), *Political Theory and Animal Rights* (London: Pluto, 1990), pp. 127–9. It is often claimed that this is merely the denial of citizenship rights to one class of persons. Such a view is misleading for it is tantamount to establishing two classes of persons, those who share in the operation of their life and those who do not so share. Both classes have the formal protection of law with respect to their life. On the rare occasions that members of the *polis* had their citizenship removed their lives were not forfeit, nor was open season declared on them.

54. Anna Laetitia Aikin Barbauld, 'An Address to the Opposers of the Repeal of the Corporation and Test Acts, Dissenter Papers (Aikin), London: 1790, British Museum 4106, f. 11, see p. 117 below.

55. See e.g. Michael Foucault, *The Archaeology of Knowledge* (London: Tavistock, 1972).

56. Barbauld, 'An Address to the Opposers of Repeal'.

57. 'Resolutions in the Minute Book of the London Corresponding Society', 2 April 1792. Place Papers, British Museum MSS 27812.

58. Ibid.

59. Jean-Jacques Rousseau, 'The Social Contract' [1762], in J-J. Rousseau, *The Social Contract and Discourses* (London: Dent, 1913), book 1. See p. 170 below.

60. Abraham Lincoln, 'The Gettysburg Address', 19 November. 1863. See pp. 152-3 below.

61. Karl Marx, 'On the Jewish Question' [1843–4], in *Selected Essays by Karl Marx*, tr. H.J. Stenning (London: Leonard Parsons, 1926), p. 84. See p. 140 below.

62. Ibid., p. 85.

63. J. Muirhead and H.J. Hetherington, *Social Purpose: A Contribution to a Philosophy of Civic Society* (London: George Allen and Unwin, 1922), p. 97.

64. T.H. Green, 'Has the Citizen Rights Against the State?' in *Lectures on the Principles of Political Obligation, Works of Thomas Hill Green*. Vol. II: *Philosophical Works* (London, Longmans, Green and Co., 1900), see p. 158 below.

65. Ibid. p. 159.

66. Henry Jones, *Principles of Citizenship* (London: Macmillan, 1919), p. viii.

67. Ibid.

68. Ibid. p. 51.

69. John MacCun, *Ethics of Citizenship* (Glasgow: James Maclehose and Sons, 1894). See p. 163 below.

70. Ibid.

71. Harold J. Laski, *The Recovery of Citizenship* (London: Ernest Benn, 1928), p. 3. See p. 168 below.

72. Ibid.

73. I refer of course to the much vaunted 'Citizens' Charter', the 'big idea' that reduces the possible richness of the idea of civic virtue to better service for consumers.

74. Laski, *The Recovery of Citizenship* see p. 168 below.

75. Bernard Mandeville, *The Fable of the Bees or Private Vices, Publick Benefits* [1XXX], vol. 1 (Oxford: Clarendon Press, 1924), p. 24.

76. Laski, see p. 170 below.

77. Alasdair MacIntyre, *After Virtue: a Study in Moral Theory* (London: Duckworth, 1981), p. 245.

78. T.H. Marshall, 'Citizenship and Social Class', [1950], in T. H. Marshall, *Citizenship and Social Class* (London: Pluto Press, 1991) see p. 175 below.

79. Joseph Mazzini, 'On the Duties of Man', [1860], in *Joseph Mazzini: a Memoir by E.A.V.* (London: Henry S. King, 1875), pp. 274–5.

80. T. H. Marshall, *Citizenship and Social Class*, see p. 176 below.

81. Ibid.

82. T.H. Marshall, 'General Survey of Changes in Social Stratification in the Twentieth Century', in *Transactions of the Third World Congress of Sociology*, vol. III (1956), p. 13.

83. James Frazer, *The Golden Bough: A Study in Magic and Religion* (London: Macmillan, 1925), p. 269.

84. Friedrich Nietzsche, *Thus Spoke Zarathustra* [1883], part 1, in R.J. Hollingdale (ed.), *A Nietzsche Reader* (Harmondsworth: Penguin, 1977), p. 204.

Part II

The Beginnings of Citizenship

1. The First Citizen

Solon c.640–559 BC

I gave to the mass of the people such rank as befitted their need,
I took not away their honour, and I granted naught to their greed;
But those who were rich in power, who in wealth were glorious and great,
I bethought me that naught should befall them unworthy their splendour
    and state;
And I stood with my shield outstretched, and both were safe in its sight.
And I would not that either should triumph, when the triumph was not
    with right.

But thus will the people best the voice of their leaders obey,
When neither too slack is the rein, nor violence holdeth the sway;
For satiety breedeth a child, the presumption that spurns control,
When riches too great are poured upon men of unbalanced soul.

So they came in search of plunder, and their cravings knew no bound,
Every one among them deeming endless wealth would here be found,
And that I with glozing smoothness hid a cruel mind within.
Fondly then and vainly dreamt they; now they raise an angry din,
And they glare askance in anger, and the light within their eyes
Burns with hostile flames upon me. Yet therein no justice lies.
All I promised, fully wrought I with the gods at hand to cheer,
Naught beyond of folly ventured. Never to my soul was dear
With a tyrant's force to govern, nor to see the good and base
Side by side in equal portion share the rich home of our race.

Wherefore I freed the racked and tortured crowd
From all the evils that beset their lot,
Thou, when slow time brings justice in its train,
O mighty mother of the Olympian gods,
Dark Earth, thou best canst witness, from those breasts
I swept the pillars broad-cast planted there,
And made thee free, who hadst been slave of yore.
And many a man whom fraud or law had sold
Far from his god-built land, an outcast slave,
I brought again to Athens; yea, and some,
Exiles from home though debt's oppressive load,
Speaking no more the dear Athenian tongue,
But wandering far and wide, I brought again;
And those that here in vilest slavery

Couched 'neath a master's frown, I set them free,
Thus might and right were yoked in harmony,
Since by the force of law I won my ends
And kept my promise. Equal laws I gave
To evil and to good, with even hand
Drawing straight justice for the lot of each.
But had another held the goad as I,
One in whose heart was guile and greediness,
He had not kept the people back from strife.
For had I granted, now what pleased the one,
Then what their foes devised within their hearts,
Of many a man this state had been bereft.
Therefore I took me strength from every side
And turned at bay like a wolf among the hounds.

> From 'The Fragments of Solon', fragments nos 6–9 reported by Aristotle in
> *Aristotle on the Athenian Constitution* [329–325 BC], tr. F.G. Kenyon (London:
> George Bell and Sons, 1981), pp. 18–20, and in 'The Fragments of Solon's
> Poems' in Ivan M. Linforth, *Solon the Athenian* (Berkeley, Calif.: University of
> California Publications in Classical Philology, vol. 6, 1919), pp. 135–9.

2. I made the Crooked Straight

Solon c. 640–559 BC

The destruction of our city will not be brought about through a decree
of Zeus or by the volition of the sacred and immortal gods. We have a
proud protector in Pallas Athena, intrepid daughter of a courageous
father who holds her defending arms over us. Rather it is the people
themselves and the deceitful and self-seeking demagogues they follow
who would ruin our majestic city with lack of restraint and devotion to
money. They are fated to endure much harm for their shameful conduct,
for they understand not how to control their laden appetites, nor,
gratified with the delight provided by the feast, to continue their
enjoyment sedately and peaceably. They have surrended to the inducement of devious ways and so have become wealthy. They have wasted
the riches of the temple, have squandered public assets, and plundered
like hoodlums one from another. They have ignored the firm foundations
of divine Justice, who, though now quiet, is mindful of all that is now
happening and that which has happened in times gone by. In due time
undoubtedly she will come to seek appropriate penalties. Even at this
time there is a plague descending on the entire township from which
perhaps no one will escape. Many of our people have come into a
humiliating and degrading slavery; slavery awakens from its slumber
conflict and internal quarrel; and conflict kills so many in the splendour

of their youth. It is as if our cherished city were the quarry of foreign adversaries, for she is being swiftly destroyed and spent in clandestine intrigues which are the enjoyment of those mendacious men.

These are the depravities which pursue us here in our city. In the meantime our destitute and impoverished are, in vast amounts, burdened with dishonourable restraints and sold into servitude in lands far away. When evil falls upon public life its scourge invades the private lives of all men. A man who thinks it can be escaped by hiding within the jurisdiction and confines of his own home is not secure, for even his house fails to furnish him with security. Such public evil vaults over the wall of his courtyard, however high that wall may be and finds him out, even should he turn and run and conceal himself in the deepest recesses of his own apartments.

These things my heart has urged me to instruct the Athenians, and to direct them to see that discord works greater damage to the community than any other cause. I have shown that a spirit of justice and principle, however, brings about order and concord, and places restraints upon the depraved and corrupt. I have shown how to make the things that are rough smooth, to check the desires that are excessive, dim the gleam of reckless conceit, wither the first blossom of barbarous illusions and make crooked judgments straight. A spirit of justice and principle arrests conceited conduct, thwarts acts of insurrection and ends the wrath of rancorous struggle so that sober judgment and wisdom always hold sway between people.

Demosthenes, *De falsa legatione* [4th century BC], 254. The recension used here is fragment 12 from 'The Fragments of Solon's Poems' in Ivan M. Linforth *Solon the Athenian* (Berkeley, Calif.: University of California Publications in Classical Philology, vol. 6, 1919), pp. 141–3.

3. On Solon

Plutarch (Ploutarchos) c. AD 46 – c. 120

Solon ... was a man of the people and of modest station; yet he in no wise acted short of his real power, relying as he did only on the wishes of the citizens and their confidence in him ...

Soon, however, they perceived the advantages of his measure, ceased from their private fault-finding, and offered a public sacrifice, which they called Seisaetheia, or *Disburdenment*. They also appointed Solon to reform the constitution and make new laws, laying no restrictions whatever upon him, but putting everything into his hands, magistracies, assemblies, courts-of-law, and councils. He was to fix the property qualification for each of these, their numbers, and their times of meeting, abrogating and maintaining existing institutions at his pleasure.

In the first place, then, he repealed the laws of Draco, all except those concerning homicide, because they were too severe and their penalties too heavy. For one penalty was assigned to almost all transgressions, namely death, so that even those convicted of idleness were put to death, and those who stole salad or fruit received the same punishment as those who committed sacrilege or murder. Therefore Demades, in later times, made a hit when he said that Draco's laws were written not with ink, but blood. And Draco himself, they say, being asked why he made death the penalty for most offences, replied that in his opinion the lesser ones deserved it, and for the greater ones no heavier penalty could be found.

In the second place, wishing to leave all the magistracies in the hands of the well-to-do, as they were, but to give the common people a share in the rest of the government, of which they had hitherto been deprived, Solon made an appraisement of the property of the citizens. Those who enjoyed a yearly increase of *five hundred measures* (wet and dry), he placed in the first class, and called them Pentakosiomedimnoi; the second class was composed of those who were able to keep a horse, or had a yearly increase of three hundred measures, and they were called Hippada Telountes, since they *paid a Knight's tax*; the members of the third class, whose yearly increase amounted to two hundred measures (wet and dry together), were called Zeugitai. All the rest were called Thetes; they were not allowed to hold any office, but took part in the administration only as members of the assembly and as jurors. This last privilege seemed at first of no moment, but afterwards proved to be of the very highest importance, since most disputes finally came into the hands of these jurors. For even in cases which Solon assigned to the magistrates for decision, he allowed also an appeal to a popular court when any one desired it. Besides, it is said that his laws were obscurely and ambiguously worded on purpose to enhance the power of the popular courts. For since parties to a controversy could not get satisfaction from the laws, the result was that they always wanted jurors to decide it, and every dispute was laid before them, so that they were in a manner masters of the laws. And he himself claims the credit for this in the following words:

For to the common people I gave so much power as is sufficient,
Neither robbing them of dignity, nor giving them too much;
And those who had power, and were marvellously rich,
Even for these I contrived that they suffered no harm,
I stood with a mighty shield in front of both classes,
And suffered neither of them to prevail unjustly.'

Moreover, thinking it his duty to make still further provision for the weakness of the multitude, he gave every citizen the privilege of entering suit in behalf of one who had suffered wrong. If a man was assaulted, and suffered violence or injury, it was the privilege of any one who had the ability and the inclination, to indict the wrong-doer and prosecute him. The law-giver in this way rightly accustomed the citizens, as member of one body, to feel and sympathize with one another's wrongs. And we are told of a saying of his which is consonant with this law. Being asked, namely, what city was best to live in, 'That city,' he replied, 'in which those who are not wronged, no less than those who are wronged, exert themselves to punish the wrong-doers.'

Reprinted by permission of the publishers and the Loeb Classical Library from Plutarch, 'Solon' [c. AD 100], tr. Bernadotte Perrin, *Plutarch's Lives*, vol. 1 (Cambridge, Mass.: Harvard University Press, 1914) pp.447–55.

4. The Funeral Oration

Pericles c. 490–429 BC

Most of my predecessors in this place have commended him who made this speech part of the law, telling us that it is well that it should be delivered at the burial of those who fall in battle ...

... since our ancestors have stamped this custom with their approval, it becomes my duty to obey the law and to try to satisfy your several wishes and opinions as best I may ...

... what was the road by which we reached our position, what the form of government under which our greatness grew, what the national habits out of which it sprang; these are questions which I may try to solve before I proceed to my panegyric upon these men ...

Our constitution does not copy the laws of neighbouring states; we are rather a pattern to others than imitators ourselves. Its administration favours the many instead of the few; this is why it is called a democracy. If we look to the laws, they afford equal justice to all in their private differences; if to social standing, advancement in public life falls to reputation for capacity, class considerations not being allowed to interfere with merit; nor again does poverty bar the way, if a man is able to serve the state, he is not hindered by the obscurity of his condition. The freedom which we enjoy in our government extends also to our ordinary life. There, far from exercising a jealous surveillance over each other, we do not feel called upon to be angry with our neighbour for doing what he likes, or even to indulge in those injurious looks which cannot fail to be offensive, although they inflict no positive penalty. But all this ease in our private relations does not make us lawless as citizens. Against this fear is our chief safeguard, teaching us to obey the magistrates and the laws, particularly such as regard the protection of the injured, whether they are actually on the statute book, or belong to that code which, although unwritten, yet cannot be broken without acknowledged disgrace ...

We throw open our city to the world, and never by alien acts exclude foreigners from any opportunity of learning or observing, although the eyes of an enemy may occasionally profit by our liberality; trusting less in system and policy than to the native spirit of our citizens; while in education, where our rivals from their very cradles by a painful discipline seek after manliness, at Athens we live exactly as we please, and yet are just as ready to encounter every legitimate danger ...

We cultivate refinement without extravagance and knowledge without effeminacy; wealth we employ more for use than for show, and place the real disgrace of poverty not in owning to the fact but in declining the struggle against it. Our public men have, besides politics, their private affairs to attend to, and our ordinary citizens, though occupied with the pursuits of industry, are still fair judges of public matters; for, unlike any other nation, regarding him who takes no part in these duties not as unambitious but as useless, we Athenians are able to judge at all events if we cannot originate, and instead of looking on discussion as a stumbling-block in the way of action, we think it an indispensable preliminary to any wise action at all. Again, in our enterprises we present the singular spectacle of daring and deliberation, each carried to its highest point, and both united in the same persons; although usually decision is the fruit of ignorance, hesitation of reflexion. But the palm of courage will surely be adjudged most justly to those, who best know the difference between hardship and pleasure and yet are never tempted to shrink from danger. In generosity we are equally singular, acquiring our friends by conferring not by receiving favours. Yet, of course, the doer of the favour is the firmer friend of the two, in order by continued kindness to keep the recipient in his debt; while the debtor feels less keenly from the very consciousness that the return he makes will be a payment, not a free gift. And it is only the Athenians who, fearless of consequences, confer their benefits not from calculations of expediency, but in the confidence of liberality.

In short, I say that as a city we are the school of Hellas; while I doubt if the world can produce a man, who where he has only himself to depend upon, is equal to so many emergencies, and graced by so happy a versatility as the Athenian ...

The admiration of the present and succeeding ages will be ours, since we have not left our power without witness, but have shown it by mighty proofs ...

Comfort, therefore, not condolence, is what I have to offer to the parents of the dead who may be here. Numberless are the chances to which, as they know, the life of man is subject; but fortunate indeed are they who draw for their lot a death so glorious as that which has caused your mourning, and to whom life has been so exactly measured as to terminate in the happiness in which it has been passed. Still I know that this is a hard saying, especially when those are in question of whom you will constantly be reminded by seeing in the homes of others blessings of which once you also boasted: for grief is felt not so much for the want of what we have never known, as for the loss of that to which we have been long accustomed. Yet you who are still of an age to beget children must bear up in the hope of having others in their stead; not only will they help you to forget those whom you have lost, but will be to the state at once a reinforcement and a security; for never can a fair or just policy be expected of the citizen who does not, like his fellows, bring to the decision the interests and apprehensions of a father. While those of you who have passed your prime must congratulate yourselves with the thought that the best part of your life was fortunate, and that the brief span that remains will be cheered by the fame of the departed. For it is only the love of honour that never grows old; and honour it is, not gain, as some would have it, that rejoices the heart of age and helplessness...

My task is now finished. I have performed it to the best of my ability, and in word, at least, the requirements of the law are now satisfied. If deeds be in question, those who are here interred have received part of their honours already, and for the rest, their children will be brought up till manhood at the public expense: the state thus offers a valuable prize, as the garland of victory in this race of valour, for the reward both of those who have fallen and their survivors. And where the rewards for merit are greatest, there are found the best citizens.

Thucydides, *History of the Peloponnesian War* [431 BC], tr. Richard Crawley (London: Dent, 1910), book II, ch. VI, nos 35–47, pp. 120–8.

5. What is a City?

Aristotle 384–322 BC

Every one who inquires into the nature of government, and what are its different forms, should make this almost his first question, What is a city? ...

... As a city is a collective body, and, like other wholes, composed of many parts, it is evident our first inquiry must be, what a citizen is: for a city is a certain number of citizens. So that we must consider whom we ought to call citizen, and who is one; for this is often doubtful: for every one will not allow that this character is applicable to the same person; for that man who would be a citizen in a republic would very often not be one in an oligarchy. We do not include in this inquiry many of those who acquire this appellation out of the ordinary way, as honorary persons, for instance, but those only who have a natural right to it.

Now it is not residence which constitutes a man a citizen; for in this sojourners and slaves are upon an equality with him; nor will it be sufficient for this purpose, that you have the privilege of the laws, and may plead or be impleaded, for this all those of different nations, between whom there is a mutual agreement for that purpose, are allowed; although it very often happens, that sojourners have not a perfect right therein without the protection of a patron, to whom they are obliged to apply, which shows that their share in the community is incomplete. In like manner, with respect to boys who are not yet enrolled, or old men who are past war, we admit that they are in some respects citizens, but not completely so, but with some exceptions, for these are not yet arrived to years of maturity, and those are past service; nor is there any difference between them. But what we mean is sufficiently intelligible and clear, we want a complete citizen, one in whom there is no deficiency to be corrected to make him so. As to those who are banished, or infamous, there may be the same objections made and the same answer given. There is nothing that more characterises a complete citizen than having a share in the judicial and executive part of the government.

With respect to offices, some are fixed to a particular time, so that no person is, on any account, permitted to fill them twice; or else not till some certain period has intervened; others are not fixed, as a juryman's, and a member of the general assembly: but probably some one may say these are not offices, nor have the citizens in these capacities any share in the government; though surely it is ridiculous to say that those who have the principal power in the state bear no office in it. But this objection is of no weight, for it is only a dispute about words; as there is no general term which can be applied both to the office of a juryman and a member of the assembly. For the sake of distinction, suppose we call it an indeterminate office: but I lay it down as a maxim, that those are citizens who could exercise it. Such then is the description of a citizen who comes nearest to what all those who are called citizens are ...

Hence it is clear that the office of a citizen must differ as governments do from each other: for which reason he who is called a citizen has, in a democracy, every privilege which that station supposes ... he who has a right to a share in the judicial and executive part of government in any city, him we call a citizen of that place; and a city, in one word, is a collective body of such persons sufficient in themselves to all the purposes of life ...

After what has been said, it follows that we should consider whether the same virtues which constitute a good man make a valuable citizen, or different; and if a particular inquiry is necessary for this matter we must first give a general description of the virtues of a good citizen; for as a sailor is one of those who make up a community, so is a citizen, although the province of one sailor may be different from another's (for one is a rower, another a steersman, a third a boatswain, and so on, each having their several appointments), it is evident that the most accurate description of any one good sailor must refer to his peculiar abilities, yet there are some things in which the same description may be applied to the whole crew, as the safety of the ship is the common business of all of them, for this is the general centre of all their cares: so also with respect to citizens, although they may in a few particulars be very different, yet there is one care common to them all, the safety of the community, for the community of the citizens composes the state; for which reason the virtue of a citizen has necessarily a reference to the state. But if there are different sorts of governments, it is evident that those actions which constitute the virtue of an excellent citizen in one community will not constitute it in another; wherefore the virtue of such a one cannot be perfect: but we say, a man is good when his virtues are perfect; from whence it follows, that an excellent citizen does not possess that virtue which constitutes a good man. Those who are any ways doubtful concerning this question may be convinced of the truth of it by examining into the best formed states: for, if it is impossible that a city should consist entirely of excellent citizens (while it is necessary that every one should do well in his calling, in which consists his excellence, as it is impossible that all the citizens should have the same qualifications) it is impossible that the virtue of a citizen and a good man should be the same; for all should possess the virtue of an excellent citizen: for from hence necessarily arise the perfection of the city: but that every one should possess the virtue of a good man is impossible, without all the citizens in a well-regulated state were necessarily virtuous.

... that man is an animal naturally formed for society, and that therefore, when he does not want any foreign assistance, he will of his own accord desire to live with others; not but that mutual advantage induces them to it, as far as it enables each person to live more agreeably; and this is indeed the great object not only to all in general, but also to each individual: but it is not merely matter of choice, but they join in society also, even that they may be able to live, which probably is not without some share of merit, and they also support civil society.

... in all political governments which are established to preserve and defend the equality of the citizens it is held right to rule by turns. Formerly, as was natural, every one expected that each of his fellow-citizens should in his turn serve the public, and thus administer to his private good, as he himself when in office had done for others; but now

every one is desirous of being continually in power, that he may enjoy the
advantage which he makes of public business and being in office; as if
places were a never-failing remedy for every complaint, and were on that
account so eagerly sought after.

It is evident, then, that all those governments which have a common
good in view are rightly established and strictly just, but those who have in
view only the good of the rulers are all founded on wrong principles, and
are widely different from what a government ought to be, for they are
tyranny over slaves, whereas a city is community of freemen.

... The doubt then which we have lately proposed, with all it consequences, may be settled in this manner; it is necessary that the freemen
who compose the bulk of the people should have absolute power in
some things; but as they are neither men of property, nor act uniformly
upon principles of virtue, it is not safe to trust them with the first
offices in the state, both on account of their iniquity and their ignorance; from the one of which they will do what is wrong, from the other
they will mistake: and yet it is dangerous to allow them no power or
share in the government; for when there are many poor people who are
incapable of acquiring the honours of their country, the state must
necessarily have many enemies in it ...

It seems, then, requisite for the establishment of a state, that all, or at
least many of these particulars should be well canvassed and inquired into;
and that virtue and education may most justly claim the right of being
considered as the necessary means of making the citizens happy ...

Now, in general, a citizen is one who both shares in the government
and also in his turn submits to be governed; their condition, it is true, is
different in different states: the best is that in which a man is enabled to
choose and to persevere in a course of virtue during his whole life, both in
his public and private state.

Aristotle, *The Politics of Aristotle* [*c.* 334 BC], tr. William Ellis (London: Dent,
1912), pp. 66–8, 71–2, 76–8, 85–6, 90, 92.

6. Against Timocrates

Demosthenes c. 383–322 BC

I am sure that you would all agree, if asked, that all evil-doers ought to
be punished; but I will try to satisfy you that this malefactor in
particular deserves punishment for introducing a law detrimental to the
common people. A thief, or a cutpurse, or any rogue of that sort, in the
first place really injures only the man who encounters him; it is out of

his power to strip everybody, or steal everybody's property; and in the second place, he brings disgrace on no one's reputation or manner of life but his own. But if a man introduces a law by which unlimited license and immunity is granted to those who seek to defraud their fellow-citizens, he is guilty in respect of the whole city, and he brings disgrace upon everybody; for an infamous statute, when ratified, is a discredit to the government that enacted it and an injury to everyone who lives under it ...

Well, men of Athens, you hold in your power to-day this man, who has not done that deed in secret, but after beguiling and deceiving you has openly enacted a law that does not merely throw open but demolishes the prison, and that includes in that destruction the courts of justice as well ...

... there seems to me to be truth in an observation once made, as we are told, in this court, that all wise men regard laws as the character of the State. Therefore we should take pains that they be accounted as good as possible, and we should punish those who debase and pervert them; for, if they are impaired by your neglect, you will lose that high distinction, and will create an unfavourable reputation for your city. If you are justified in praising Solon and Draco, although you can credit neither of them with any public service except that they enacted beneficial and well-conceived statutes, it is surely right that you should visit men whose enactments are contrary to the spirit of those lawgivers with indignation and chastisement. But as to Timocrates I know that he brought in this law chiefly for his private advantage, because he felt that many of his political acts in your city deserve imprisonment.

I would also like to repeat to you a saying attributed to Solon, when he was prosecuting a man who had carried an undesirable law. We are told that, after stating his other charges, he observed that in all, or nearly all, states there is a law that the penalty for any man who debases the currency is death. He proceeded to ask the jury whether they thought that a just and good law; and when the jury replied that they did, he said that in his opinion money had been invented by private persons for private transactions, but laws were the currency of the State; and therefore if a man debased that currency, and introduced counterfeit, the jury had graver reason to abhor and punish that man than one who debased the currency of private citizens.

... no nation that uses bad laws or permits the debasement of existing laws has ever escaped the consequence. Now that is the accusation to which Timocrates stands open to-day, and he may justly receive from you the punishment that is adequate to his guilt.

Reprinted by permission of the publishers and the Loeb Classical Library from Demosthenes, 'Against Timocrates', [c. 350 BC] tr. J.H. Vince, *Demosthenes*, vol. III (Cambridge, Mass.: Harvard University Press, 1935).

7. The Duty of a Ruler towards the Citizens

Marcus Tullius Cicero 106–43 BC

... it appears that nothing is more agreeable and suited to the nature and minds of men than undisguised openness, truth, and sincerity. Next to this love and affection for truth, there follows in the soul an impatient desire and inclination to pre-eminence; so that whoever has the genuine nature of a man in him, will never endure to be subject to another, unless he be one that instructs or advises, or is invested with a just and lawful authority for the benefit of the public: whence there arises a greatness of soul, which sets it above all the petty concerns and trifling enjoyments of this present world. It is another, and that too no mean prerogative of our reasonable nature, that man alone can discern all the beauties of order and decency, and knows how to govern his words and actions in conformity to them. It is he alone that, of all the creatures, observes and is pleased with the beauty, gracefulness, and symmetry of parts in the objects of sense; which nature and reason observing in them, from thence take occasion to apply the same also to those of the mind; and to conclude that beauty, consistency, and regularity, should be much more kept up in our words and actions; and therefore command us, that nothing be done that is effeminate or unbecoming; and that so strict a guard be kept over every thought and action, as that no indecency be either conceived or practised by us. From these inclinations and instincts of nature arises and results that honesty we are seeking for; which, however little valued and esteemed it may be, is nevertheless virtuous and amiable in itself; and which we may justly say, though it were commended by no one, is yet in its own nature truly commendable...

Those who design to be partakers in the government should be sure to remember those two precepts of Plato; first, to make the safety and interest of their citizens the great aim and design of all their thoughts and endeavours, without ever considering their own personal advantage; and, secondly, so to take care of the whole collective body of the republic, as not to serve the interest of any one party, to the prejudice or neglect of all the rest: for the government of a state is much like the office of a guardian or trustee; which should always be managed for the good of the pupil, and not of the persons to whom he is entrusted; and those men who, whilst they take care of one, neglect or disregard another part of the citizens, do but occasion sedition and discord, the most destructive things in the world to a state: whence it comes to pass, that while some take part with the popular faction, and others make their court to every great one, there are but very few left who are concerned for the benefit and good of the whole. From this root have sprung many grievous dissensions amongst the Athenians; and not only tumults, but even destructive civil wars in our own republic; things which a worthy and truly brave citizen, and one who deserves to hold the reins of the government, will shun and detest; and will give himself so to the service of the public, as to aim at no riches or power for himself; and will so take care of the whole community, as not to pass over any one part of it. Such a one will scorn, by the mean arts of calumny and a false accusation, to bring others into hatred and disrepute with the people, but will always adhere to what is just and honest, and never be drawn from it, whatever offence may be taken by others; nay, will rather part with his life itself, than do anything that is contrary to the virtues I have mentioned. Eager ambition, and contending for honour, is of all things most ruinous and destructive to a state; concerning which Plato had said admirably well, – 'that for men to contend and fall out with one another, about which should be chief in the management of the state, is just as if the ship's crew should go together by the ears about who should be master or pilot of the vessel.' And the same philosopher has given us this for a rule – 'that only those men should be reckoned enemies who have taken up arms in opposition to the republic; not those who would govern it after their own schemes.' Such was the dissension between P. Africanus and Q. Metellus, without any great bitterness or animosities between them. Some people think it the part of a brave and heroic spirit to show heat of anger and passion against an adversary; but what they say is by no means to be regarded; for it is certain, on the other hand, that nothing is more laudable, nothing more worthy of a great and brave person, than clemency, meekness, and gentleness of spirit. In cities that are free, and where all men in common enjoy the same privileges, courtesy, and affability, and a calm and undisturbed temper of mind are peculiarly requisite; for to fret on every unseasonable visit, or at every impertinent and troublesome petitioner, makes a man sour and morose in his humour; which, as it brings no manner of good to himself, so it gets him the hatred and ill-will of others. But though meekness and clemency be laudable virtues, yet no farther than as they leave room for a just severity, whenever the occasions of the public require it; without which a city can never be well governed. Now every reproof and chastisement in the first place, should be always free from contumelious language, and not inflicted for the sake of the person chastising or reproving another, but for the good and advantage of the whole republic. Diligent care should be taken, in the next place, that the penalty be proportioned to the nature of the crime; and that some do not pass without ever being questioned, while others are punished for the same misdemeanours. But of all things, anger should be excluded in punishing: for whoever comes to this work in a passion, will never observe that due mediocrity, which equally abstains from too much and too little, so strictly required by the Peripatetic schools; and they have very good reason indeed to require it; but then I cannot but wonder they should commend anger, and say, Nature has given it us to good ends and purposes: for that in truth ought in no case to be allowed of; and it were heartily to be wished that the governors of a state would, in this particular, be like the laws themselves, which punish offenders according to justice, without being anyways guided by passion ...

Cicero, *The Offices* [46–44 BC], tr. T. Cockman (London: George Routledge and Sons, 1893), book 1, nos IV, XXV, pp. 14, 52–4.

8. Remember This Day

Marcus Tullius Cicero 106–43 BC

So, citizens of Rome, since a public thanksgiving has been voted to be held at all the sacred couches, keep the festal days with your wives and children. Many honours justly deserved have often ere now been paid to the immortal gods, but surely none more justly due to them than these. For you have been rescued from a most barbarous and heartrending destruction, and rescued without bloodshed, without slaughter, without an army, without a prolonged struggle; by civil weapons, and with me in my civil capacity as your only leader and general, you have won the day ...

... In this war, the greatest and most barbarous within the memory of man, a war such as no uncivilised government has ever carried on with its own subjects, a war in which Lentulus, Catalina, Cethegus, and Cassius, deliberately adopted the principle that all persons, whose safety would be secured by the safety of the city, should be reckoned as enemies, in this war, I say, men of Rome, I have conducted myself so as to preserve the safety of all of you, and though your enemies had imagined that only so many of the citizens would survive as should have escaped the indiscriminate massacre, and only so much of the city, as could not have been reached by the flames, I have kept both the city and the citizens absolutely untouched and unharmed.

For these important services, citizens of Rome, I do not require from you any reward of merit, any outward sign of honour, any memorial of my renown, except the eternal remembrance of this day. In your hearts and there alone I desire that all my triumphs, all my honourable distinctions, all the memorials of my glory, all the outward signs of my fame, may be laid up and stored. No material reward can please me, nothing that is lifeless and mute, nothing in short that men less worthy can obtain. By your remembrance, men of Rome, our deeds will be kept fresh, in the phrases of ordinary life they will be perpetuated, in the records of literature they will reach maturity and lasting strength. I understand that the same period, never to end I hope, will now witness the prolonged welfare of the city and the prolonged remembrance of my consulship; and I know that at the same moment two citizens appeared in Rome [Cn. Pompeius Magnus and Cicero himself were both born in 106 BC], the one destined to extend the bounds of your empire not to the ends of the earth but to the limits of the sky, the other to preserve from destruction the seat and centre of that same extended empire.

But since the fate of the services which I have rendered, is very different from the fortune of those who have had the charge of foreign wars, in that I have to live with those whom I have vanquished and subdued, while they left their enemies behind them either slain or completely crushed, it is your duty, citizens of Rome, if it is right that others profit by their deeds, to take precautions that I may not some day be a loser by mine. I took precautions that the wicked and abominable designs of violent men might be no injury to you: it is yours to take precautions that they may not injure me. However, men of Rome, to me myself no injury can now be done by them. There is a strong defence to be found in the favour of the good citizens, and this I have secured for ever; there is a strong authority in the state, and this will always silently defend me; there is great strength in the voice of conscience, and those who disregard its warning, when they wish to assail me, will betray themselves. There is moreover in us, men of Rome, a spirit that will not allow us to submit to violence from any man, but on the contrary will make us always anticipate attack by challenging all bad men. But if these foes that are of our own household, foiled in their assault on you, direct their whole violence against me alone, you will have to consider, men of Rome, what fate you wish to be hereafter the reward of those who for your welfare have exposed themselves to unpopularity and perils of every kind. For me personally what is there which can now increase the good to be derived from life, especially as I see no higher step to which I can to mount either in the distinctions which you confer or in the fame that virtue brings? I will assuredly, men of Rome, devote myself to the task of preserving and keeping bright in private life the work which I have done as consul, so that if any unpopularity has been incurred by my efforts to preserve the state, it may recoil on those who excite it, and redound only to my honour. In short, I will so behave in public life as to bear in mind always what I have done, and to prove that my success should be ascribed to my own efforts and not to accident. Do you, citizens of Rome, since it is now evening, worship Jupiter, the great protector of this city and of you, and disperse to your own homes; and though the danger is now averted, still keep watch and ward as carefully as on the former night. I will provide that you may not be obliged to watch much longer, and that you may be able to remain in perpetual tranquillity.

Cicero, 'Third Catilinarian Speech' [63 BC], in *The Speeches of M. Tullius Cicero against Cataline and Antony and for Murena and Milo*, tr. Herbert E.D. Blakiston (London: Methuen, 1894), nos 23, 24, pp. 54-9.

9. The World is our City

Lucius Annaeus Seneca (The Younger) c. 5 BC – AD 65

For as some men pass the day in seeking the sun and in exercise and care of the body, and as athletes find it is most profitable by far to devote the greater part of the day to the development of their muscles and the strength to which alone they have dedicated themselves; so for you, who are training your mind for the struggle of political life, by far the most desirable thing is to be busy at one task. For, whenever a man has the set purpose to make himself useful to his countrymen and all mortals, he both gets practice and does service at the same time when he has placed himself in the very midst of active duties, serving to the best of his ability the interests both of the public and of the individual. 'But because,' he continues, 'in this mad world of ambition where chicanery so frequently twists right into wrong, simplicity is hardly safe, and is always sure to meet with more that hinders than helps it, we ought indeed to withdraw from the forum and public life, but a great mind has an opportunity to display itself freely even in private life; nor, just as the activity of lions and animals is restrained by their dens, is it so of man's, whose greatest achievements are wrought in retirement. Let a man, however, hide himself away bearing in mind that, wherever he secretes his leisure, he should be willing to benefit the individual man and mankind by his intellect, his voice and his counsel. For the man that does good service to the state is not merely he who brings forward candidates and defends the accused and votes for peace and war, but he also who admonishes young men, who instils virtue into their minds, supplying the great lack of good teachers, who lays hold upon those that are rushing wildly in pursuit of money and luxury, and draws them back, and, if he accomplishes nothing else, at least retards them – such a man performs a public service even in private life. Or does he accomplish more who in the office of praetor, whether in cases between citizens and foreigners or in cases between citizens, delivers to suitors the verdict his assistant has formulated, than he who teaches the meaning of justice, of pity, of endurance, of bravery, of contempt of death, of knowledge of the gods, and how secure and free is the blessing of a good conscience? If, then, the time that you have stolen from public duties is bestowed upon studies, you will neither have deserted, nor refused, your office. For a soldier is not merely one who stands in line and defends the right or the left wing, but he also who guards the gates and fills, not an idle, but a less dangerous, post, who keeps watch at night and has charge of the armoury; these offices, though they are bloodless, yet count as military service. If you devote yourself to studies, you will have escaped all your disgust at life, you will not long for night to come because you are weary of the light, nor will you be either burdensome to yourself or useless to others; you will attract many to friendship and those that gather about you will be the most excellent. For virtue, though obscured, is never concealed, but always gives signs of its presence; whoever is worthy will trace her out by her footsteps. But if we give up society altogether and, turning our backs upon the human race, live with our thoughts fixed only upon ourselves, this solitude deprived of every interest will be followed by a want of something to be accomplished. We shall begin to put up some buildings, to pull down others, to thrust back the sea, to cause waters to flow despite the obstacles of nature, and shall make ill disposition of the time which Nature has given us to be used. Some use it sparingly, others wastefully; some of us spend it in such a way that we are able to give an account of it, others in such a way – and nothing can be more shameful – that we have no balance left. Often a man who is very old in years has no evidence to prove that he has lived a long time other than his age.'

To me, my dearest Serenus, Athenodorus seems to have surrendered too quickly to the times, to have retreated too quickly. I myself would not deny that sometimes one must retire, but it should be a gradual retreat without surrendering the standards, without surrendering the honour of a soldier; those are more respected by their enemies and safer who come to terms with their arms in their hands. This is what I think Virtue and Virtue's devotee should do. If Fortune shall get the upper hand and shall cut off the opportunity for action, let a man not straightway turn his back and flee, throwing away his arms and seeking some hiding-place, as if there were anywhere a place where Fortune could not reach him, but let him devote himself to his duties more sparingly, and, after making choice, let him find something in which he may be useful to the state. Is he not permitted to be a soldier? Let him seek public office. Must he live in a private station? Let him be a pleader. Is he condemned to silence? Let him help his countrymen by his silent support. Is it dangerous even to enter the forum? In private houses, at the public spectacles, at feasts let him show himself a good comrade, a faithful friend, a temperate feaster. Has he lost the duties of a citizen? Let him exercise those of a man. The very reason for our magnanimity in not shutting ourselves up within the walls of one city, in going forth into intercourse with the whole earth, and in claiming the world as our country, was that we might have a wider field for our virtue.

Reprinted by permission of the publishers and the Loeb Classical Library from Seneca, 'On Tranquillity of Mind' [c. AD 50], tr. John William Basore, *Moral Essays* (Cambridge, Mass.: Harvard University Press, 1928) pp. 223–9.

10. A Citizen of Rome

St Luke First century AD

... the Jews from Asia seeing Paul in the temple stirred up the crowd, and laid their hands on him crying out, 'Men, Israelites, help, this is the man who is everywhere teaching against the people and the law.' ... And the whole of the people together in the city were aroused, and laid hold of Paul and dragged him outside the temple.

While they were trying to kill him the tribune heard that all Jerusalem was in confusion. At once taking soldiers and centurions he ran down to the people and they seeing the tribune with the soldiers ceased beating Paul. Drawing near to him the tribune laid hold of Paul and ordered him bound with two chains. He inquired of him who he was and what he had done ...

Paul replied, 'I am a man, indeed am a Jew, a Tarsian, of Cilicia a citizen of no mean city and I beg of you permit me to speak to the people.'

With permission Paul ... addressed the people ...

And the people heard him ... and lifted up their voice saying, 'Take from the earth such a man; for it is not fitting for him to live.'

And they shouted and tore garments and threw dust in the air.

The tribune commanded Paul to be brought into the fort, bidding him to be examined with scourges, so that he might then fully know what crime the people were calling against him. As they stretched him with thongs Paul said to the centurion standing by him, 'If a man is a Roman citizen and uncondemned is it lawful for you to scourge him?'

Hearing this the centurion approached the tribune and reported to him saying, 'What are you about to do? – for this man is a Roman.'

And approaching Paul the tribune said to him, 'Tell me, are you a Roman?'

And he said, 'Yes.'

The tribune responded, 'I acquired this citizenship for a large sum of money.'

So Paul said, 'But I indeed have been born a citizen.'

Those about to examine him moved immediately away from him as did the Tribune who was afraid knowing fully that he had bound a Roman citizen.

Acts XXII, 21–9.

11. A New Covenant

St Paul First century AD

Behold the days are coming,
says the Lord,
when I will bring into being
over the household of Israel
and over the household of Juda
a new covenant.

This will not be like the covenant
which I made with their fathers
on the day I took their hand
to lead them out of Egypt,
for they did not continue in my covenant,
so I disregarded them,
says the Lord.

In this covenant,
which I will make with the household of Israel
after those days,
says the Lord,
I will put my laws into their minds,
and inscribe them on their hearts
and I will be to them their God
and they shall be to me my people.

And in no manner may they teach each man
their fellow citizen
and each man their brother,
saying: Know the Lord,
because all will know me
from the smallest to the greatest of them.

Hebrews, VIII, 8–11.

12. The City is Superior to the Citizen

Epictetus c. AD 50

Examine who you are. In the first place, a man: that is, one who hath nothing superior to the faculty of choice; but all things subject to this; and this itself unenslaved, and unsubjected, to anything. Consider, then, from what you are distinguished by reason. You are distinguished from wild beasts: you are distinguished from cattle. Besides, you are a citizen of the world, and a part of it; not a subservient, but a principal part. You are capable of comprehending the divine economy; and of considering the connections of things. What then doth the character of a citizen promise? To hold no private interest; to deliberate of nothing as a separate individual, but like the hand or the foot, which, if they had reason, and comprehended the constitution of nature, would never pursue, or desire, but with a reference to the whole. Hence the philosophers rightly say, that, if a wise and good man could foresee what was to happen, he would help forward sickness and death, and mutilation, to himself; being sensible that these things are appointed from the order of the universe, and that the whole is superior to a part, and the city to the citizen. But, since we do not foreknow what is to happen, it becomes our duty to adhere to what is more naturally adapted to our option: for, amongst other things, we were born for this.

> Epictetus, 'The Discourses' [*c.* AD 50], in *The Moral Discourses of Epictetus*, tr. Elizabeth Carter (London: Dent, 1910), p. 85.

13. Harm to the Citizen is Harm to the State

Marcus Aurelius Antoninus   AD 121–80

Let it not be in any man's power to say truly of thee that thou art not simple or that thou art not good; but let him be a liar whoever shall think anything of this kind about thee; and this is altogether in thy power. For who is he that shall hinder thee from being good and simple? Do thou only determine to live no longer, unless thou shalt be such. For neither does reason allow [thee to live], if thou art not such.

What is that which as to this material [our life] can be done or said in the way most conformable to reason? For whatever this may be, it is in thy power to do it or to say it; and do not make excuses that thou art hindered. Thou wilt not cease to lament till thy mind is in such a condition, that, what luxury is to those who enjoy pleasure, such shall be to thee in the matter which is subjected and presented to thee the doing of the things which are conformable to man's constitution; for a man ought to consider as an enjoyment everything which it is in his power to do according to his own nature. And it is in his power everywhere. Now it is not given to a cylinder to move everywhere by its own motion, nor yet to water nor fire, nor to anything else which is governed by nature or an irrational soul, for the things which check them and stand in the way are many. But intelligence and reason are able to go through everything that opposes them, and in such manner as they are formed by nature and as they choose.

Place before thy eyes this facility with which the reason will be carried through all things, as fire upwards, as a stone downwards, as a cylinder down an inclined surface, and seek for nothing further. For all other obstacles either affect the body only which is a dead thing; or, except through opinion and the yielding of the reason itself, they do not crush nor do any harm of any kind; for if they did, he who felt it would immediately become bad. Now in the case of all things which have a certain constitution, whatever harm may happen to any of them, that which is so affected becomes consequently worse; but in the like case, a man becomes both better, if one may say so, and more worthy of praise by making a right use of these accidents. And finally remember that nothing harms him who is really a citizen, which does not harm the state; nor yet does anything harm the state, which does not harm law [order]; and of these things which are called misfortunes not one harms law. What then does not harm law does not harm either state or citizen.

Marcus Aurelius Antoninus, 'Meditations' [AD 169–80] in *The Thoughts of the Emperor M. Aurelius Antoninus*, tr. George Long (London: Bell and Daldy, 1862), pp. 178–80.

Part III

The Christian Citizen

1. Epistle to Diognetus

Anon c. AD 200

1. For the distinction between Christians and other men, is neither in country nor language nor customs. 2. For they do not dwell in cities in some place of their own, nor do they use any strange variety of dialect, nor practise an extraordinary kind of life. 3. This teaching of theirs has not been discovered by the intellect or thought of busy men, nor are they the advocates of any human doctrine as some men are. 4. Yet while living in Greek and barbarian cities, according as each obtained his lot, and following the local customs, both in clothing and food and in the rest of life, they show forth the wonderful and confessedly strange character of the constitution of their own citizenship. 5. They dwell in their own fatherlands, but as if sojourners in them; they share all things as citizens, and suffer all things as strangers. Every foreign country is their fatherland, and every fatherland is a foreign country. 6. They marry as all men, they bear children, but they do not expose their offspring. 7. They offer free hospitality, but guard their purity. 8. Their lot is cast 'in the flesh,' but they do not live 'after the flesh.' 9. They pass their time upon the earth, but they have their citizenship in heaven. 10. They obey the appointed laws, and they surpass the laws in their own lives. 11. They love all men and are persecuted by all men. 12. They are unknown and they are condemned. They are put to death and they gain life. 13. 'They are poor and make many rich'; they lack all things and have all things in abundance. 14. They are dishonoured, and are glorified in their dishonour, they are spoken evil of and are justified. 15. 'They are abused and give blessing,' they are insulted and render honour. 16. When they do good they are buffeted as evil-doers, when they are buffeted they rejoice as men who receive life. 17. They are warred upon by the Jews as foreigners and are persecuted by the Greeks, and those who hate them cannot state the cause of their enmity.

1. To put it shortly what the soul is in the body, that the Christians are in the world. 2. The soul is spread through all members of the body, and Christians throughout the cities of the world. 3. The soul dwells in the body, but is not of the body, and Christians dwell in the world, but are not of the world. 4. The soul is invisible, and is guarded in a visible body, and Christians are recognised when they are in the world, but their religion remains invisible. 5. The flesh hates the soul, and wages war upon it, though it has suffered no evil, because it is prevented from gratifying its pleasures, and the world hates the Christians though it has suffered no evil, because they are opposed to its pleasures. 6. The soul loves the flesh which hates it and the limbs, and Christians love those that hate them. 7. The soul has been shut up in the body, but itself

sustains the body; and Christians are confined in the world as in a prison, but themselves sustain the world. 8. The soul dwells immortal in a mortal tabernacle, and Christians sojourn among corruptible things, waiting for the incorruptibility which is in heaven. 9. The soul when evil treated in food and drink becomes better, and Christians when buffeted day by day increase more. 10. God has appointed them to so great a post and it is not right for them to decline it.

Reprinted by permission of the publishers and the Loeb Classical Library, the 'Epistle to Diognetus', [2nd or 3rd century AD], tr. Kirsopp Lake, *The Apostolic Fathers*, (Cambridge, Mass.: Harvard University Press, 1913) pp. 359–62.

2. The Two Cities

St. Augustine of Hippo AD 354–430

What produces peace, and what discord, between the heavenly and earthly cities.

But the families which do not live by faith seek their peace in the earthly advantages of this life; while the families which live by faith look for those eternal blessings which are promised, and use as pilgrims such advantages of time and of earth as do not fascinate and divert them from God, but rather aid them to endure with greater ease, and to keep down the number of those burdens of the corruptible body which weigh upon the soul. Thus the things necessary for this mortal life are used by both kinds of men and families alike, but each has its own peculiar and widely different aim in using them. The earthly city, which does not live by faith, seeks an earthly peace, and the end it proposes, in the well-ordered concord of civic obedience and rule, is the combination of men's wills to attain the things which are helpful to this life. The heavenly city, or rather the part of it which sojourns on earth and lives by faith, makes use of this peace only because it must, until this mortal condition which necessitates it shall pass away. Consequently, so long as it lives like a captive and a stranger in the earthly city, though it has already received the promise of redemption, and the gift of the Spirit as the earnest of it, it makes no scruple to obey the laws of the earthly city, whereby the things necessary for the maintenance of this mortal life are administered; and thus, as this life is common to both cities, so there is a harmony between them in regard to what belongs to it. But, as the earthly city has had some philosophers whose doctrine is condemned by the divine teaching, and who, being deceived either by their own conjectures or by demons, supposed that many gods must be invited to take an interest in human affairs, and assigned to each a separate function and a separate department, – to one the body, to another the soul; and in the body itself, to one the head, to another the neck, and each of the other members to one of the gods; and in like manner, in the soul, to one god the natural capacity was assigned, to another education, to another anger, to another lust; and so the various affairs of life were assigned, – cattle to one, corn to another, wine to another, oil to another, the woods to another, money to another, navigation to another, wars and victories to another, marriages to another, births and fecundity to another, and other things to other gods: and as the celestial city, on the other hand, knew that one God only was to be worshipped, and that to Him alone was due that service which the Greeks call λ a τ ρ ε i a, and which can be given only to a god, it has come to pass that the two cities could not have common laws of religion, and that the heavenly city has been compelled in this matter to dissent, and to become obnoxious to those who think differently, and to stand the brunt of their anger and hatred and persecutions, except in so far as the minds of their enemies have been alarmed by the multitude of the Christians and quelled by the manifest protection of God accorded to them. This heavenly city, then, while it sojourns on earth, calls citizens out of all nations, and gathers together a society of pilgrims of all languages, not scrupling about diversities in the manners, laws, and institutions whereby earthly peace is secured and maintained, but recognising that, however various these are, they all tend to one and the same end of earthly peace. It therefore is so far from rescinding and abolishing those diversities, that it even preserves and adopts them, so long only as no hindrance to the worship of the one supreme and true God is thus introduced. Even the heavenly city, therefore, while in its state of pilgrimage, avails itself of the peace of earth, and, so far as it can without injuring faith and godliness, desires and maintains a common agreement among men regarding the acquisition of the necessaries of life, and makes this earthly peace bear upon the peace of heaven; for this alone can be truly called and esteemed the peace of the reasonable creatures, consisting as it does in the perfectly ordered and harmonious enjoyment of God and of one another in God. When we shall have reached that peace, this mortal life shall give place to one that is eternal, and our body shall be no more this animal body which by its corruption weighs down the soul, but a spiritual body feeling no want, and in all its members subjected to the will. In its pilgrim state the heavenly city possesses this peace by faith; and by this faith it lives righteously when it refers to the attainment of that peace every good action towards God and man; for the life of the city is a social life.

Augustine, 'City of God' [413–16], in Marcus Dods (ed.), *The Works of Aurelius Augustine, Bishop of Hippo*, vol. II: *The City of God* (Edinburgh: T. and T. Clarke, 1871–6), book XIX, ch. 17, pp. 326–8.

3. Human Law May Be Perverted

St Thomas Aquinas 1224–74

The Philosopher says that the 'intention of every lawgiver is to make good citizens.'

I answer that, As stated above, ... a law is nothing else than a dictate of reason in the ruler by which his subjects are governed. Now the virtue of any subordinate thing consists in its being well subordinated to that by which it is regulated; thus we see that the virtue of the irascible and concupiscible faculties consists in their being obedient to reason; and accordingly 'the virtue of every subject consists in his being well subjected to his ruler,' as the Philosopher says. But every law aims at being obeyed by those who are subject to it. Consequently it is evident that the proper effect of law is to lead its subjects to their proper virtue; and since virtue is 'that which makes its subject good,' it follows that the proper effect of law is to make those to whom it is given good, either simply or in some particular respect. For if the intention of the lawgiver is fixed on true good, which is the common good regulated according to divine justice, it follows that the effect of the law is to make men good simply. If, however, the intention of the lawgiver is fixed on that which is not simply good, but useful or pleasurable to himself, or in opposition to divine justice, then the law does not make men good simply, but in respect to that particular government. In this way good is found even in things that are bad of themselves: thus a man is called a good robber because he works in a way that is adapted to his end.

Virtue is twofold, ... acquired and infused. Now the fact of being accustomed to an action contributes to both, but in different ways; for it causes the acquired virtue, while it disposes to infused virtue, and pre-serves and fosters it when it already exists. And since law is given for the purpose of directing human acts as far as human acts conduce to virtue, so far does law make men good. Wherefore the Philosopher says in the second book of the *Politics* [*Ethics* ii] that 'lawgivers make men good by habituating them to good works.'

It is not always through perfect goodness of virtue that one obeys the law, but sometimes it is through fear of punishment, and sometimes from the mere dictate of reason, which is a beginning of virtue.

The goodness of any part is considered in comparison with the whole; hence Augustine says that 'unseemly is the part that harmonizes not with the whole.' Since then every man is a part of the state, it is impossible that a man be good unless he be well proportionate to the common good: nor can the whole be well consistent unless its parts be proportionate to it. Consequently the common good of the state cannot flourish unless the citizens be virtuous, at least those whose business it is to govern. But it is enough for the good of the community that the other citizens be so far virtuous that they obey the commands of their rulers. Hence the Philosopher says that 'the virtue of a sovereign is the same as that of a good man, but the virtue of any common citizen is not the same as that of a good man.'

A tyrannical law, through not being according to reason, is not a law, absolutely speaking, but rather a perversion of law; and yet in so far as it is something in the nature of a law, it aims at the citizens being good. For all it has in the nature of a law consists in its being an ordinance made by a superior to his subjects, and aims at being obeyed by them, which is to make them good, not simply, but with respect to that particular government.

St Thomas Aquinas, 'Summa Theologica' [1266–73] in Dino Bigongiari (ed.), *The Political Ideas of St. Thomas Aquinas* (Indianapolis, Ind.: Bobbs-Merrill, 1974), pp. 24–6.

4. Private Gain, Public Harm

Desiderius Erasmus 1466–1536

Let me give a few words on the defense of peace and concord to those of you who actually despise war. Peace is not to be found in various leagues or confederations of men, which are ofttimes the very source and cause of wars. We must look for peace by purging the very sources of war, false ambitions and evil desires. As long as individuals serve their own personal interests, the common good will suffer. No one achieves what he desires if the methods employed be evil. The princes should use their wisdom for the promotion of what is good for the entire populace. The measure of their majesty, happiness, renown, and riches should be what actually makes great men outstanding. Let their attitude toward the common good be that of a father toward his family. The mark of a great and noble king is that he so acts and governs as to make his subjects honest, content, and wealthy. In this he should respect the wealth of his richer citizens, the freedom of his city-dwellers, and above all he should take care that peace flourish in all places. His subordinates should imitate their king and take special care that the common good of all be protected. In this way they will insure their own office of state. Will a king that is of this mind hand over the money of his subjects to strange and barbarous mercenaries? Will he expose them to famine and hunger to provide pay for hired captains? Will he risk the lives of his people with many dangers? We do not think so.

In his performance of kingly duties let him bear always in mind that as a man he is dealing with fellow men, that as a free citizen he is dealing with free citizens, and above all that as a Christian he is dealing with fellow Christians. The citizenry on their part must act in such a manner that their respect for the king be motivated also by the interests of the common good. No ruler can expect more than this. Consent and approval on the part of the citizens will be a curb to the aspirations of the prince. For both the ruler and the subject private gain should not be a consideration.

Desiderius Erasmus, 'The Complaint of Peace' [1517], in *The Essential Erasmus*, tr. John P. Dolan (New York: New American Library, 1964), pp. 193–4.

Part IV

The Italian Revival

1. A Monarch is the Servant of All

Dante Aligheri 1265–1321

Freedom ... is the greatest gift conferred by God on human nature; for through it we have our felicity here as men, through it we have our felicity elsewhere as deities. And if this be so, who would not agree that the human race is best disposed when it has fullest use of this principle [of freedom]? But it is under a monarch that it is most free. As to which we must know that that is free which exists 'for the sake of itself and not of some other,' as the Philosopher has it in his work, *De Simpliciter Ente*. For that which exists for the sake of something else is conditioned by that for the sake of which it exists, as a road is conditioned by the goal. It is only when a monarch is reigning that the human race exists for its own sake, and not for the sake of something else. For it is only then that perverted forms of government are made straight, to wit democracies, oligarchies, and tyrannies, which force the human race into slavery, (as is obvious to whosoever runs through them all), and that government is conducted by kings, aristocrats ... and zealots for the people's liberty. For since the monarch has love of men in the highest degree, as already indicated, he will desire all men to be made good, which cannot be under perverted rulers. Whence the Philosopher [Aristotle] in his *Politics* says, 'Under a perverted government a good man is a bad citizen, but under a right one, a good man and a good citizen are convertible terms.' And such right governments purpose freedom, to wit that men should exist for their own sakes. For the citizens are not there for the sake of the consuls, nor the nation for the sake of the king, but conversely, the consuls for the sake of the citizens, the king for the sake of the nation. For just as the body politic is not established for the benefit of the laws, but the laws for the benefit of the body politic, so too they who live under the law are not ordained for the benefit of the legislator, but rather he for theirs, as saith the Philosopher again in what has been left by him on the present matter. Hence it is clear that, albeit the consul or king be masters of the rest as regards the way, yet as regards the end they are their servants; and the monarch most of all, for he must assuredly be regarded as the servant of all. Hence it may begin to appear at this point how the monarch is conditioned in laying down the laws by the end set before him.

Therefore the human race is best disposed when under a monarchy. Whence it follows that for the well-being of the world the existence of a monarchy is necessary.

Dante Aligheri, De Monarchia [1309–13] tr. Philip H. Wickstead, (London: Dent, 1904), book 1, chs XII–XIII, pp. 158–60.

2. Only Citizens May Make Laws

Marsilius of Padua c. 1275–1342

A citizen I define in accordance with Aristotle in the *Politics*, Book III, Chapters 1, 3, and 7, as one who participates in the civil community in the government or the deliberative or judicial function according to his rank. By this definition, children, slaves, aliens, and women are distinguished from citizens, although in different ways. For the sons of citizens are citizens in proximate potentiality, lacking only in years. The weightier part of the citizens should be viewed in accordance with the honorable custom of polities, or else it should be determined in accordance with the doctrine of Aristotle in the *Politics*, Book VI, Chapter 2.

Having thus defined the citizen and the weightier part of the citizens, let us return to our proposed objective, namely, to demonstrate that the human authority to make laws belongs only to the whole body of the citizens or to the weightier part thereof. Our first proof is as follows. The absolutely primary human authority to make or establish human laws belongs only to those men from whom alone the best laws can emerge. But these are the whole body of the citizens, or the weightier part thereof, which represents that whole body; since it is difficult or impossible for all person to agree upon one decision, because some men have a deformed nature, disagreeing with the common decision through singular malice or ignorance. The common benefit should not, however, be impeded or neglected because of the unreasonable protest or opposition of these men. The authority to make or establish laws, therefore, belongs only to the whole body of the citizens or to the weightier part thereof ...

That at which the entire body of the citizens aims intellectually and emotionally is more certainly judged as to its truth and more diligently noted as to its common utility. For a defect in some proposed law can be better noted by the greater number than by any part thereof, since every whole, or at least every corporeal whole, is greater in mass and in virtue than any part of it taken separately. Moreover, the common utility of a law is better noted by the entire multitude, because no one knowingly harms himself. Anyone can look to see whether a proposed law leans toward the benefit of one or a few persons more than of the others or of the community, and can protest against it. Such, however, would not be the case were the law made by one or a few persons, considering their own private benefit rather than that of the community ...

That law is better observed by every citizen which each one seems to have imposed upon himself. But such is the law which is made through the hearing and command of the entire multitude of the citizens. The first proposition of this prosyllogism is almost self-evident; for since 'the state is a community of free men,' as is written in the *Politics*, Book III, Chapter 4, every citizen must be free, and not undergo another's despotism, that is, slavish dominion. But this would not be the case if one or a few of the citizens by their own authority made the law over the whole body of citizens. For those who thus made the law would be despots over the others, and hence such a law, however good it was, would be endured only with reluctance, or not at all, by the rest of the citizens, the more ample part. Having suffered contempt, they would protest against it, and not having been called upon to make it, they would not observe it. On the other hand, a law made by the hearing or consent of the whole multitude, even though it were less useful, would be readily observed and endured by every one of the citizens, because then each would seem to have set the law upon himself, and hence would have no protest against it, but would rather tolerate it with equanimity. The second proposition of the first syllogism I also prove in another way, as follows. The power to cause the laws to be observed belongs only to those men to whom belongs coercive force over the transgressors of the laws. But these men are the whole body of citizens or the weightier part thereof. Therefore, to them alone belongs the authority to make the laws.

The principal conclusion is also proved as follows. That practical matter whose proper establishment is of greatest importance for the common sufficiency of the citizen in this life, and whose poor establishment threatens harm for the community, must be established only by the whole body of the citizens ...

For men came together to the civil community in order to attain what was beneficial for sufficiency of life, and to avoid the opposite. Those matters, therefore, which can affect the benefit and harm of all ought to be known and heard by all, in order that they may be able to attain the beneficial and to avoid the opposite ...

The authority to make the laws belongs, therefore, to the whole body of citizens or to the weightier part thereof, for precisely the opposite reason. For since all the citizens must be measured by the law according to due proportion, and no one knowingly harms or wishes injustice to himself, it follows that all or most wish a law conducing to the common benefit of the citizens ...

Objections will be made to our above statements, to the effect that the authority to make or establish laws does not belong to the whole body of the citizens.

... it is easy to refute the objections whereby one might try to prove that the making of the law does not pertain to the whole body of the citizens or the weightier multitude thereof but rather to a certain few.

As for the first objection, that the authority to make laws does not belong to those who in most cases are vicious and undiscerning, this is granted. But when it is added that the whole body of citizens is such, this must be denied. For most of the citizens are neither vicious nor undiscerning most of the time; all or most of them are of sound mind and reason and have a right desire for the polity and for the things necessary for it to endure, like laws and other statutes or customs, as was shown above. For although not every citizen nor the greater number of the citizens be discoverers of the laws, yet every citizen can judge of what has been discovered and proposed to him by someone else, and can discern what must be added, subtracted, or changed ...

Nor is this position invalidated by those who say that the wise, who are few, can discern what should be enacted with regard to practical matters better than can the rest of the multitude. For even if this be true, it still does not follow that the wise can discern what should be enacted better than can the whole multitude, in which the wise are included together with the less learned. For every whole is greater than its part both in action and in discernment ...

... even though it be easier to harmonize the views of fewer persons than of many, it does not follow that the views of the few, or of the part, are superior to those of the whole multitude, of which the few are a part. For the few would not discern or desire the common benefit equally as well as would the entire multitude of the citizens. Indeed, it would be insecure, as we have already shown, to entrust the making of the law to the discretion of the few. For they would perhaps consult therein their own private benefit, as individuals or as a group, rather than the common benefit ...

... although the laws can be better made by the wise than by the less learned, it is not therefore to be concluded that they are better made by the wise alone than by the entire multitude of citizens, in which the wise are included. For the assembled multitude of all of these can discern and desire the common justice and benefit to a greater extent than can any part of that multitude taken separately, however prudent that part may be.

Hence those do not speak the truth who hold that the less learned multitude impedes the choice and approval of the true or common good; rather, the multitude is of help in this function when it is joined to those who are more learned and more experienced. For although the multitude cannot by itself discover true and useful measures, it can nevertheless discern and judge the measures discovered and proposed to it by others, as to whether they should be added to, or subtracted from, or completely changed, or rejected ...

It is hence appropriate and highly useful that the whole body of citizens entrust to those who are prudent and experienced the investigation, discovery, and examination of the standards, the future laws or statutes, concerning civil justice and benefit, common difficulties or burdens, and other similar matters ....

After such standards, the future laws, have been discovered and diligently examined, they must be laid before the assembled whole body of citizens for their approval or disapproval, so that if any citizen thinks that something should be added, subtracted, changed, or completely rejected, he can say so, since by this means the law will be more usefully ordained. For, as we have said, the less learned citizens can sometimes perceive something which must be corrected in a proposed law even though they could not have discovered the law itself. Also, the laws thus made by the hearing and consent of the entire multitude will be better observed, nor will anyone have any protest to make against them ...

> Marsilius of Padua, 'Discourse One' [1324] in *Defensor Pacis*, tr. A. Gewirth, Mediaeval Academy Reprints for Teaching, vol. 6 (Toronto: University of Toronto Press, 1980), chs XII, XIII, pp. 45–9, 51–5.

3. To Know the City

Leonardo Bruni 1369–1444

An eminent place among the precepts of moral philosophy which define and teach human conduct belongs to those concerned with cities and their government and conservation. For this is a philosophy whose whole purpose is to bring happiness to human beings. If it is a good thing for a single individual to attain happiness, how much more glorious it would be for a whole city to achieve the good life. The more widely good is distributed, the more divine it must be. And since the human being is a feeble animal, and does not have sufficiency and perfection in himself, and must get this from civil society, certainly no branch of philosophy can be more appropriate to him than to know what a city is and what a republic is, and not to be ignorant of the causes by which civil society may be preserved or destroyed ...

> Leonardo Bruni, 'Preface to the Translation of Aristotle's *The Politics*', in *The Humanism of Leonardo Bruni: Selected Texts*, tr. Gordon Griffiths, James Hankins and David Thompson, Medieval and Renaissance Texts and Studies, vol. 46 (Binghamton, NY: State University of New York, 1978), p. 162.

4. In Praise of the City of Florence

Leonardo Bruni 1369–1444

But as this city is to be admired for its foreign policy, so it is for its internal organization and institutions. Nowhere else is there such order, such elegance, such symmetry. For just as there is a proportion among strings which, when they have been tightened, produces a harmony from the different pitches, than which there is nothing sweeter or more agreeable to the ear; so all the parts of this prudent city are so tempered that the resulting whole commonwealth fits together in a way that brings pleasure to the mind and eyes of men for its harmony. There is nothing in it that is out of order, nothing that is ill-proportioned, nothing that is out of tune, nothing that is uncertain. Everything has its place, and this is not only fixed, but correct in relation to the others. Offices, magistracies, courts and ranks are all separate. But they are separated in such a way that they are in harmony with the whole commonwealth, as tribunes were with respect to the general.

First, every consideration is given to providing that justice shall be held sacred in the city, for without that, no city can exist or deserve the name; secondly, that there be liberty, without which this people never thought life was worth living. Toward these two ideals together, as toward a kind of ensign and haven, all the institution and legislative acts of this republic are directed.

It is for the sake of justice that the magistracies were established, and endowed with sovereign authority and the power to punish criminals, and above all so that they may see to it that no one's power in the city will be above the law. Accordingly all private citizens, as persons of lesser rank, are enjoined to obey the magistrates and to honor their symbols of office. But lest these defenders of the law, who have been put into positions of the highest authority, should get the idea that what had been offered them was an opportunity to tyrannize over the citizens rather than to protect them, and lest a measure of freedom should be lost as a result of their persecution of others, many precautions have been taken.

... it is believed by this city that what affects the many it was not fitting in law or reason to decide except by the will of the many. In this way liberty flourishes and justice is devotedly served in this city, since nothing can be carried out in response to the desire of one or another man against the will of so many. Instead, men like these offer their advice to the commonwealth, ratify and repeal laws and determine what is equitable.

For the actual pronunciation of sentences on the basis of these laws, however, and for the execution of sentences, there are lesser magistracies; and for this purpose foreigners from far away are called into the city to serve in the place of citizens, not because the citizens would not know how to do it (for they do do it in foreign cities every day), but so that carrying out the judicial function should not become a cause of mutual hatred and enmity among the citizens. For there are many who, deceived by excessive love of self, claim more authority for themselves than the laws permit; who, even if the judgment has been right, pursue complaints against the magistracy. It was seen to be an especially serious matter for a citizen in a free city to impose a capital sentence upon another citizen; for if he did so, however justly, he would be viewed by the other citizens as polluted and obnoxious. It is for this reason that the judges are recruited from a long distance, and that laws governing their conduct are prescribed from which they may not depart in any way. For they must agree to them under oath, and when they leave office, they must, like brokers, submit an account of their performance in office to the people. Thus in every sphere the people and liberty rule.

In order, however, for everyone in such a large city to secure his rights the more easily, and to be sure that some citizens would not be left unprotected by justice and the laws while magistracies were preoccupied with other citizens' affairs, certain guilds have been given cognizance and power of judgment over their own members, for example, merchants, bankers, and certain others, some of whom even have the right of coercion over their own men. There are other magistracies, established for either public or pious purposes, among which are the tax masters and the directors of the treasury, and the guardians of orphans and of orphan property – a magistracy which serves both a public and a private purpose, and was conceived by a generous city in a spirit that was both pious and beneficial.

But of all the many and distinguished magistracies in this city, none is more illustrious nor does any have a more splendid origin or purpose than the captains of the good party (*optimarum partium duces*) ...

... this magistracy possesses enormous authority in the city. For it has been given the position of a sentinel and guardian, as it were, to see to it that the commonwealth shall not deviate from the course followed by our ancestors, and that the government of the commonwealth should not fall into the hands of men of opposing sentiments. Thus the function performed by the censors in Rome, by the council of the Areopagus in Athens and by the ephors in Sparta, is performed in Florence by the captains of the party. In other words, it is from among these citizens who love the republic that the leaders are chosen to serve as guardians of the republic.

So excellent and caring is the government of this city under these magistracies that one may say that there never was a household with better discipline under a watchful *paterfamilias*. Accordingly no one here can suffer injury, nor does anyone lose his property involuntarily. The courts and magistracies are always ready to hear cases; the courtroom and the supreme court are open. There is the freest opportunity in this city to file a complaint against persons of any rank, but under laws that are prudent and salutary and always accessible to afford relief. There is no place on earth in which justice is fairer for all. For nowhere does such liberty flourish, nor such a balanced relationship between greater and lesser. For here, too, this city's prudence – greater perhaps than that of any other – is noteworthy. For when the powerful, relying on their wealth, were seen to be injuring and disdaining the weak, the republic itself undertook the defense of the powerless and secured their persons and property by the establishment of higher penalties upon the former. In accordance with reason the city decided that it was fitting that different penalties should be imposed on different ranks of men; and that it should provide those in need with greater help out of its resources of skill and justice. Thus a certain balance among the various ranks was created, since the great can rely on their power, the small on the commonwealth, and both on the fear of punishment to deter transgressors. From this the saying was born, which we hear most frequently hurled against the powerful, for when they threaten something, the cry goes up at once: 'I, too, am a Florentine citizen!' By this saying they seem to be attesting and publicly warning that no one should despise anybody on account of his weakness, nor continue to threaten injury by exploiting his own power; that the situation of everyone is the same, since those with less power will be avenged by the commonwealth itself.

Not only citizens, but aliens as well are protected by this commonwealth. It suffers injury to be done to no man, and endeavors to see that everyone, citizen or alien, shall receive the justice that is owing to him. This same justice and equity, while fostering good human relations among citizens, since nobody can be too puffed up or hold the rest in contempt, at the same time really encourages courtesy to all men. As for the rectitude of their lives and the high level of their morality, who could do them justice in the time remaining?

There are in this city the most talented men, who easily surpass the limits of other men in whatever they do. Whether they follow the military profession, or devote themselves to the task of governing the commonwealth, or to certain studies or to the pursuit of knowledge, or to commerce – in everything they undertake and in every activity they far surpass all other mortals, nor do they yield first place in any field to any other nation. They are patient in their labor, ready to meet danger, ambitious for glory, strong in counsel, industrious, generous, elegant, pleasant, affable, and above all, urbane.

Leonardo Bruni, 'Laudatio' (1403–4) in *The Humanism of Leonardo Bruni: Selected Texts*, tr. Gordon Griffiths, James Hankins and David Thompson, Leonardo Bruni, [1403–4], in Medieval and Renaissance Texts and Studies, vol. 46 (Binghamton, NY: State University of New York, 1987), pp. 116–21.

5. Funeral Oration

Leonardo Bruni 1369–1444

There was an ancient law of Solon (in my opinion, a very wise man) which was also confirmed and warranted by the custom of his very wise city: it provided that citizens who had died fighting for their country should be accorded, after the private ceremonies, a public funeral with a splendid display of words as well as outward things. The latter were devoted to the funeral procession, the former to the praise of those who had perished ...

What moved me to recall this celebrated and praiseworthy law was the glorious death of a distinguished man, the Florentine knight, Nanni Strozzi, who died fighting in this war which our city and the Venetians are now waging against the duke of Milan ...

This important responsibility for pronouncing the eulogy which has been intrusted to me would not seem to me a burden at all if only I had the talent and the ability to satisfy what is expected in such a glorious type of address. But I know that it is very difficult to do this worthily, and that without great talent and great eloquence one should not attempt it, especially since in a public funeral eulogy it is appropriate to include a eulogy to the city, too ...

If we begin therefore with a eulogy of his country, it will be recognized that we have chosen the right beginning for our address.

For the city in which he was born is one of the greatest and most illustrious; it is possessed of a wide dominion, and universal respect. It was without question the chief city of the Etruscans, and is second to none of the Italian cities in birth, wealth or size. To the origin of the city the two noblest and most distinguished peoples of all Italy contributed: the Etruscans, who were the ancient lords of Italy, and the Romans, whose virtue and arms enabled them to establish an empire over the world ...

What city, therefore, can be of better or nobler birth, or be better endowed with the glory of ancient forefathers? Or indeed which of the most powerful cities is to be compared with ours in this kind of distinction? Deserving also of commendation are our ancestors who, when they fell heirs to this city, established institutions and governed in such a manner that they seem to have departed as little as possible from the virtue of those from whom they were descended ... Also deserving of praise are the citizens of this present age, who have extended the city's

power even beyond what they inherited from their fathers, adding
through the exercise of virtue and arms Pisa and other large cities to
their dominion ...

But leaving behind now, or deferring, foreign affairs, let us, if I may
put it this way, look into and examine the body of the city itself.

The constitution we use for the government of the republic is
designed for the liberty and equality of indeed all the citizens. Since it is
egalitarian in all respects, it is called a 'popular' constitution. We do not
tremble beneath the rule of one man who would lord it over us, nor are
we slaves to the rule of a few. Our liberty is equal for all, is limited only
by the laws, and is free from the fear of men. The hope of attaining
office and of raising oneself up is the same for all, provided only one
put in effort and have talent and a sound and serious way of life. Virtue
and probity are required of the citizens by our city. Anyone who has
these two qualities is thought to be sufficiently well-born to govern the
republic. The pride and haughtiness of the powerful are so vehemently
hated that more severe laws have been enacted to penalize this kind of
man than there are for any other purpose. The proud were finally
conquered and compelled by the law's quite adamantine chains to bend
their necks and to humble themselves to a level beneath that of the
middle class, so that it is regarded as a great privilege to be allowed to
transfer from the category of the *grandi* into that of the *popolo*. This is
true liberty, this is fairness in a city: not to have to fear violence or
injury from any man, and for the citizens to be able to enjoy equality of
the law and a government that is equally accessible to all. But these
conditions cannot be maintained under the rule of one man or of a few.
For those who prefer royal government appear to ascribe a virtue to the
king that they grant was never present in any man. What king has there
ever been who would carry out all the acts involved in government for
the sake of his people, and desire nothing for his own sake beyond the
mere glory of the name? This is why praise of monarchy has something
fictitious and shadowy about it, and lacks precision and solidity. Kings,
the historian says, are more suspicious of the good than of the evil man,
and are always fearful of another's virtue. Nor is it very different under
the rule of the few. Thus the only legitimate constitution left is the
popular one, in which liberty is real, in which legal equity is the same
for all citizens, in which pursuit of the virtues may flourish without
suspicion. And when a free people are offered this possibility of attaining offices, it is wonderful how effectively it stimulates the talents of the
citizens. When shown a hope of gaining office, men rouse themselves
and seek to rise; when it is precluded they sink into idleness. In our
city, therefore, since this hope and prospect is held out, it is not at all
surprising that talent and industriousness should be conspicuous.

Leonardo Bruni, 'Oration for the Funeral of Nanni Strozzi' [1428], in *The Humanism of Leonardo Bruni: Selected Texts*, tr. Gordon Griffiths, James Hankins and David Thompson, Medieval and Renaissance Texts and Studies, vol. 46 (Binghamton, NY: State University of New York, 1987), pp. 121–7. Copyright: Center for Medieval and Early Renaissance Studies, SUNY, Binghamton.

Part V

Citizenship in the Emerging State

1. Tyranny is Contrary to Nature and Reason

Thomas Starkey c. 1495–1538

POLE: First this is certain, that like as in every man there is a body and also a soul in whose flourishing and prosperous state both together standeth the weal and felicity of man, so likewise there is in every commonality, city and country, as it were a politic body, and another thing also resembling the soul of man, in whose flourishing both together resteth also the true common weal. This body is nothing else, but the multitude of people the number of citizens in every commonality, city or country. The thing which is resembled to the soul, is civil order and political law administered by officials and rulers. For like as the body in every man receives his life by the virtue of the soul and is governed thereby, so does the multitude in every country receive, as it were, civil life by laws administered by good officials and wise rulers, by whom they be governed, and kept in politic order, wherefore the one may, as me seemeth, right well be compared to the body, and the other to the soul.

LUPSET: This similitude liketh me well.

POLE: Then let us go forth with the same, and we shall find by and by, that like as the weal of every man separately by himself rises of the principal things before declared, so the common weal of every country city or town similarly riseth of other things proportionally and like to the same, in the which all other particular things are comprehended. And the first of them shortly to say standeth in health strength and beauty of this body politic, and multitude of people, wherein resteth the ground and, as it were, the foundation of the common weal. For if the country be never so rich, fertile, and plentiful of all things necessary and pleasant to man's life, yet if there be of people either too few, or too many, or if they be as it were eaten, away daily devoured and consumed by common sickness and disease, there can be no image or shadow of any common weal. To the which first is required a convenient multitude and conveniently to be nourished there in the country. For whereas there be other too many people in the country, in so much that the country by no diligence nor labour of man be sufficient to nourish them and minister them food, there without doubt can be no common weal, but ever miserable penury and wretched poverty. Like as if there be of people overfew, in so much that the country may not be well tilled and occupied, nor crafts well and diligently exercised, there shall also spring thereof great penury and scarceness of all things necessary for man's life, and so then, civil life and true common weal can in no case be there maintained. Wherefore a convenient multitude meet for the place, in every country and commonality, as the matter and ground of the common weal, is first to be required of necessity ...

How be it, this ever is certain and sure among all sorts and nature of people whether the state of the commonality, be governed by a prince, by certain wise men, or by the whole multitude so long as they which have authority and rule of the state look not to their own singular profit nor to the private weal of any one party more than to the other, but refer all their council acts and deeds, to the common weal of the whole, so long, I say, the order is good, and directed to good civility, and this is good policy. But when they which have rule, corrupt with ambition, envy or malice, or any like affect, look only to their own singular weal, pleasure and profit, then this good order is turned in to high tyranny. Then is broken the rule of all good civility there can be no political rule, nor civil order the nature whereof now to perceive is, as I think, nothing hard at all. For it is a certain rule whereby the people and whole commonality, whether they be governed by a prince or common council, is ever directed in virtue and honesty. So that the end of all political rule is, to induce the multitude to virtuous living, according to the dignity of the nature of man. And so thus you have heard what thing it is that I so often speak of and call political rule, civil order and just policy ...

If all the parties of the city with love be not knit together in unity as members of one body, there can be no civility. For like as in man's mind there only is quietness and high felicity, whereas in a good body all the affects with reason do agree. So in a country city or town where there is perfect civility, there is the true common weal, whereas all the parties as members of one body be knit together in perfect love and unity, everyone doing his office and duty after such manner that, whatsoever state, office or degree, any man be of, the duty thereto pertaining with all diligence he busily fulfil, and without envy or malice to other accomplish the same. As by example their heads and rulers both spiritual and temporal to do their duty, providing always that first and above all the people may be instructed with the doctrine of Christ, fed and nourished with the spiritual food of his celestial word, ever directed thereto by all good policy, so that consequently they may quietly labour, both without outward impediment and hurt of enemies, and also without inward injury among themselves, one oppressing another with wrongs, and injury but diligently to labour procuring food and things necessary for the whole political body. And this is the office, and duty, briefly, to say of heads and rulers ...

Master Lupset, if Kings and princes in realms were by election chosen such as, of all other, for their princely virtue, were most worthey to rule, it were then very convenient they should have all such authority as is annexed to the same. But seeing they be not so, but come by succession, you see they be seldom of that sort, as I said before, but, ruled by affection, draw all things to their singular lust, vain pleasure, and inordinate will. It cannot be denied but to the common weal such authority, other usurped or by prerogative given thereto is pernicious and hurtful to the common weal, and here in our country, (freely to speak between you and me) a great destruction to our country, which hath been perceived by our forefathers days at diverse and many times, and should be also now, if we had not a noble and wise prince which is ever content to submit himself to the order of his counsel, nothing abusing his authority ...

LUPSET: Sir, this I cannot deny but that a fault there is, as me seems therein, but how it should be addressed and reformed again I cannot yet see but with much more inconvenience ensuing the same.

POLE: Well, as for that, we shall see when time and place it shall require. Now let us boldly affirm this to be a great disorder in the political rule here of our country. Seeing the kings here are taken by succession of blood, and not by free election, which is in our polity, another great fault and disorder also, and of us now specially to be noted seeing that we have purposed before, ever as a mark to shoot unto, the very and true common weal, which cannot long stand in such state whereas princes are ever had by succession of blood, specially if we give unto him such regal and princely power as we do in our country. For though sometime it may fortune such a prince to be born which will not abuse such power, yet for the most part the contrary will have place ...

LUPSET: Sir, in this matter I can scant tell you what I shall say, for on the one part when I hear your reasons me seems they are probable and like the truth, but on the other side when I look to the experience and consider the manners, customs and natures here of our country me seems the contrary, and that it should be very expedient to have our prince by succession of blood and not by election, in so much as the end of all laws and political rule is to keep the citizens in unity and peace and perfect concord among themselves. For in no country may be any greater pestilence or more pernicious than civil war sedition and discord among the parts of the political body. This is the thing that has destroyed all commonalities ... after my opinion your sentence makes a way, for what thing may be devised occasion of more strife amongst us than to chose our king by election of lords and peers of the realm? For then every man would be king, every man would judge himself as mete as another and so there should be factions and parties with great ambition, and envy, and so also at the end, ever sedition and civil war. For our people be of that nature that if they had such liberty surely they would abuse it to their own destruction. Therefore, me seemeth, foreasmuch as we be used to take our prince by succession of blood, this free election that you so praise may not be admitted.

POLE: Well Master Lupset notwithstanding that by good reason you seem to defend this custom long used in our realm and nation yet if we remember our purpose well and order of reasoning it shall be nothing hard to take away your reason at all. This you know is our purpose; to find out the best order that by prudent policy may be stabilised in our realm [and country], and to find all faults which repugne to the same, of the which this I noted to be one principal and chief. For what is more repugnant to nature, than a whole nation to be governed by the will of a prince, which ever follows his frail fantasy and unruly affectations? What is more contrary to reason than all the whole people to be ruled by him, which commonly lacks all reason. Like to the Romans whose common weal may be example to all other, which like as their consuls so likewise their kings chose ever of the best and most excellent in virtue. Like also unto Lacedemonia, and in all other noble countries of Greece, where the people were ruled by a prince, and you shall find that he was ever chosen by free election. This succession of princes by inheritance and blood was brought in by tyrannous and barbarous princes, which, as I said, is contrary to nature and all right reason, which you may see, also, more evidently, by succession in private families, wherein you see that if the son be prodigal and given to all vice and folly, the father is not bound to make him his heir, which is good policy, but hath liberty to choose him another whereas he thinketh convenient and best. Much more is it to be admitted in a realm that, if the prince be not mete to succeed his father, that then another is to be chosen by the free election of the citizens in the country. Wherefore we may this surely conclude that the best it is for the conservation of political order and just policy, a prince to be chosen by free election at liberty ...

LUPSET: Sir, you have now satisfied me right well. For now I see that, notwithstanding that it is better, as our people are affect, to have our prince by succession of blood, yet if they would live in true liberty and observe the civil life convenient to the nature of man, best it were to have him chosen by free election ...

'A Dialogue between Cardinal Pole and Thomas Lupset by T. Starkey' [1535], in J.M. Cowper (ed.), *England in the Reign of King Henry the Eighth*, part II (London: Early English Text Society, 1878), pp. 43–5, 53–5, 104–8. Some spelling has been revised and all punctuation has been added to the original MSS by subsequent editors.

2. Concerning the Citizen

Jean Bodin c. 1530–96

When the head of the family leaves the household over which he presides and joins with other heads of families in order to treat of those things which are of common interest, he ceases to be a lord and master, and becomes an equal and associate with the rest. He sets aside his private concerns to attend to public affairs. In so doing he ceases to be a master and becomes a citizen, and a citizen may be defined as a free subject dependent on the authority of another ...

I use the term *free subject*, because although a slave is as much, or more, subject to the commonwealth as is his lord, it has always been a matter of common agreement that the slave is not a citizen, and in law has no personality. This is not the case with women and children, who are free of any servile dependence, though their rights and liberties, especially their power of disposing of property, is limited by the domestic authority of the head of the household. We can say then that every citizen is a subject since his liberty is limited by the sovereign power to which he owes obedience. We cannot say that every subject is a citizen. This is clear from the case of slaves. The same applies to aliens. Being subject to the authority of another, they have no part in the rights and privileges of the community ...

Just as slaves can be slaves either by birth or by convention, so citizens can be either natural or naturalized. The natural citizen is the free subject who is a native of the commonwealth, in that both, or one or other of his parents, was born there ... The naturalized citizen is one who makes a voluntary submission to the sovereign authority of another, and is accepted by him as his subject. An honorary citizen who has been granted certain privileges such as civic rights, either as the reward of merit, or an act of grace and favour, is not properly a citizen because he does not thereby become a subject. The whole body of the citizens, whether citizens by birth, by adoption or by enfranchisement (for these are the three ways in which citizen rights are acquired) when subjected to the single sovereign power of one or more rulers, constitutes a commonwealth, even if there is diversity of laws, language, customs, religion, and race. If all the citizens are subject to a single uniform system of laws and customs they form not only a commonwealth but a commune, even though they be dispersed in divers townships, villages, or the open countryside. The town is not the commune, as some have held, any more than the house is the household, for dependants and children can live in widely separated places, yet still form a household, if they are subject to a single head of the family. The same applies to the commune. It can consist of a number of townships and villages, provided they share the same customs, as is the case with the bailliwicks of this realm. Similarly the commonwealth can include a number of communes and provinces which all have different customs. But so long as they are subject to the authority of a single sovereign, and the laws and ordinances made by it, they constitute a commonwealth ...

It is a very grave error to suppose that no one is a citizen unless he is eligible for public office, and has a voice in the popular estates, either in a judicial or deliberative capacity. This is Aristotle's view. Later he corrects himself when he observes that it only applies to popular states. But he himself said in another place that a definition is valueless unless it is of universal application ... Plutarch improved on this description when he said that citizenship implied a right to a share in the rights and privileges of a city-state, implying that he meant such a share as accorded with the standing of each, nobles, commoners, women, and children too, according to the differences of age, sex, and condition ... It must however be emphasized that it is not the rights and privileges which he enjoys which makes a man a citizen, but the mutual obligation between subject and sovereign, by which, in return for the faith and obedience rendered to him, the sovereign must do justice and give counsel, assistance, encouragement, and protection to the subject. He does not owe this to aliens ... Moreover, although a man can be a slave of more than one master, or a vassal of more than one lord provided they all hold of the same overlord, a citizen cannot be the subject of more than one sovereign, unless they are both members of a federated state. For princes are not subject to any jurisdiction which delimits their claims over their subjects, as are lords and masters in respect of their vassals and slaves. Neglect of this principle is the reason why there are so frequently frontier wars between neighbouring princes. Each claims the population of the march country as his own. These latter recognize one or other disputant as it suits them, or escape dependence on either, and in consequence are invaded and pillaged by both sides equally...

It is a generally accepted principle of public right that mere change of domicile from one country to another does not deprive the subject of his citizen rights, nor his prince of his sovereign authority over him. The case is parallel to that of the vassal who under feudal custom cannot escape the faith he owes his lord, any more than his lord can excuse himself from the obligation to protect his vassal, unless there has been agreement between them to this effect, seeing that the obligation is mutual and reciprocal. But if both parties have expressly or tacitly consented, and the prince has suffered his subject to renounce his subjection and submit to another, then the subject is no longer bound in obedience to his former sovereign ... In order then to acquire full rights of citizenship, it is not sufficient to have been domiciled for the statutory period. Letters of naturalization must also have been asked for and obtained. A settlement cannot be made on anyone unless the benefactor has offered, and the beneficiary duly accepted, the gift offered. Similarly an alien does not become a citizen, nor the subject of a foreign prince, until he has been received as such by that prince, but remains the subject of his natural prince. The same is the case if he has asked for admission to citizenship and been refused ...

It is therefore the submission and obedience of a free subject to his prince, and the tuition, protection, and jurisdiction exercised by the prince over his subject that makes the citizen. This is the essential distinction between the citizen and the foreigner. All other differences are accidental and circumstantial, though it is an almost universal rule in commonwealths that all or certain offices and benefices should be open only to citizens, and aliens debarred from them altogether ...

As for the differences that distinguish different classes of subjects from each other, they are almost as numerous as those which distinguish citizens from aliens, taking all places into account. I have referred to some, the difference between noble and commoner, adults and children, men and women. There are also distinctions of persons before the law, some being exempt from the taxes, charges, and impositions that others are subject to. In nearly every state in Europe citizens are divided into the three orders of nobles, clergy, and people. In addition to this general division there are special arrangements in certain commonwealths such as the division into gentlemen, citizens, and proletariat in Venice ... Even Plato, although he intended all his citizens to enjoy an equality of rights and privileges, divided them into the three orders of guardians, soldiers, and labourers. All this goes to show that there never was a commonwealth, real or imaginary, even if conceived in the most popular terms, where citizens were in truth equal in all rights and privileges. Some always have more, some less than the rest.

Jean Bodin, 'Six Books of the Commonwealth' [1576], in *Bodin: Six Books of the Commonwealth*, tr. and ed. M.J. Tooley, Blackwell's Political Texts (Oxford: Blackwell, 1955), pp. 18–22.

3. Citizen and Subject

Thomas Hobbes 1588–1679

... he who submits his will to the will of another, conveys to that other the right of his strength and faculties. Insomuch as when the rest have done the same, he to whom they have submitted, hath so much power, as by the terror of it he can conform the wills of particular men unto unity and concord.

Now union thus made, is called a city or civil society; and also a civil person. For when there is one will of all men, it is to be esteemed for one person; and by the word *one*, it is to be known and distinguished from all particular men, as having its own rights and properties. Insomuch as neither any one citizen, nor all of them together, (if we except him, whose will stands for the will of all), is to be accounted a city. A *city* therefore, (that we may define it), is *one person*, whose will, by the compact of many men, is to be received for the will of them all; so as he may use all the power and faculties of each particular person to the maintenance of peace, and for common defence.

But although every city be a civil person, yet every civil person is not a city; for it may happen that many citizens, by the permission of the city, may join together in one person, for the doing of certain things. These now will be civil persons; as the companies of merchants, and many other convents. But cities they are not, because they have not submitted themselves to the will of the company simply and in all things, but in certain things only determined by the city, and on such terms as it is lawful for any one of them to contend in judgment against the body itself of the sodality; which is by no means allowable to a citizen against the city. Such like societies, therefore, are civil persons subordinate to the city.

In every city, that man or council, to whose will each particular man hath subjected his will so as hath been declared, is said to have the *supreme power*, or *chief command*, or *dominion*. Which power and right of commanding, consists in this, that each citizen hath conveyed all his strength and power to that man or council; which to have done, because no man can transfer his power in a natural manner, is nothing else than to have parted with his right of resisting. Each citizen, as also every subordinate civil person, is called the *subject* of him who hath the chief command.

By what hath been said, it is sufficiently showed in what manner and by what degrees many natural persons, through desire of preserving themselves and by mutual fear, have grown together into a civil person, whom we have called a *city*. But they who submit themselves to another for fear, either submit to him whom they fear, or some other whom they confide in for protection. They act according to the first manner, who are vanquished in war, that they may not be slain; they according to the second, who are not yet overcome, that they may not be overcome. The first manner receives its beginning from natural power, and may be called the natural beginning of a city; the latter from the council and constitution of those who meet together, which is a beginning by institution. Hence it is that there are two kinds of cities; the one natural, such as the paternal and despotical; the other institutive, which may be also called political. In the first, the lord acquires to himself such citizens as he will; in the other, the citizens by their own wills appoint a lord over themselves, whether he be one man or one company of men, endued with the command in chief ...

Democracy is not framed by contract of particular persons with the *people*, but by mutual compacts of single men each with other. But hence it appears, in the first place, that the persons contracting must be in being before the contract itself. But the *people* is not in being before the constitution of government, as not being any person, but a multitude of single persons; wherefore there could then no contract pass between the people and the subject. Now, if after that government is framed, the subject make any contract with the people, it is in vain; because the people contains within its will the will of that subject, to whom it is supposed to be obliged; and therefore may at its own will and pleasure disengage itself, and by consequence is now actually free. But in the second place, that single persons do contract each with other, may be inferred from hence; that in vain sure would the city have been constituted, if the citizens had been engaged by no contracts to do or omit what the city should command to be done or omitted. Because, therefore, such kind of compacts must be understood to pass as necessary to the making up of a city, but none can be made (as is already shewed) between the subject and the people; it follows, that they must be made between single citizens, namely, that each man contract to submit his will to the will of the major part, on condition that the rest also do the like. As if every one should say thus: I give up my right unto the people for your sake, on condition that you also deliver up yours for mine ...

Thomas Hobbes, 'De Cive', [1642], in *The English Works of Thomas Hobbes of Malmesbury*, ed. Sir William Molesworth, vol. II, ch. 5 (London: John Bohn, 1841), pp. 69–71, 98–9.

4. On the Duties of Citizens

Samuel Von Pufendorf 1632–92

1. The duties of the citizens are either general or special. General duties originate from communal obligation, by which citizens are subject to civil authority. Special duties originate from particular functions given to individuals by sovereign authority.

2. The general duties of citizens are to the rulers of the state, to the entire state, or to fellow-citizens.

3. To the rulers a citizen owes respect, loyalty and obedience. Hence a citizen should, assent to the regime and think not of revolution, refrain from giving his loyalty to, or admiring or respecting, another regime; have a good and just opinion of the regime and its actions, and declare his accord.

4. A good citizen's duty towards the entire state is, to hold its welfare and safety most dear; to offer his life and property to its preservation: to advance its interests and reputation with all industry and strength of mind.

5. It is the duty of the citizen towards his fellows to live in friendship and peace with them, to be obliging and good-natured, to refrain from causing

trouble by being petulant or difficult; to refrain from envy of the advantage of others, and not to deprive them of such advantage as they may have.

6. Special duties concern, either the entire state, or a part of the state. In both cases it is a general rule that a man should refrain from undertaking any state duty for which he thinks he is unfit.

7. Advisers to the rulers of the state should keep their attention on every part of the state; that which seems in the interests of the state must be declared with skill and truth, without partiality and without unworthy motives; in all their advice they should aim at the welfare of the state and not at their own advantage; they should not indulge or flatter the evil inclinations of princes; they should not engage in factions and unlawful gatherings: it behoves them to dissimulate that which should be said, yet not reveal confidences: they should not be corruptible by foreigners, and they should not favour private business or pleasure over public business or pleasure.

8. Those appointed to perform religious duties must do so with dignity and care and profess only truth about devotion to God; by their own behaviour they should exhibit a worthy and conspicuous example to the people of that which they teach, nor by moral depravity impair the power of their teaching or divest their office of dignity.

9. Teachers appointed to instil knowledge into the minds of the citizens should not teach that which is false or noxious: the truth should be transferred in such a way so that those listening assent not from habit, but because they have been given substantial reasons; they should not teach that which tends to disturb civil society, and hold human knowledge redundant, if it provides no gain for the life of man and citizen.

10. Those charged with the supervision of justice must make access to justice available to everyone, and protect common people from domination by the more powerful; justice is to be given to the underprivileged and menial and to the strong and powerful alike; and cases not drawn out beyond what is needed; they should refrain from dishonesty, be diligent in attending to cases; every emotion that sways fair judgment should be put aside, they should be frightened of no one in doing right.

11. Commanders of the army should train soldiers with dispatch and diligence and in such a way that they are able to endure the ordeals of martial life; they should maintain military discipline, and not recklessly expose soldiers to butchery by the enemy; they should furnish grain and pay promptly, without taking any of it for themselves; they should ensure that soldiers always remain faithful to the state, and must never plot with them against the state.

12. Soldiers for their part should be satisfied with their pay; and abstain from plundering and annoying the people; they should willingly and agreeably undergo labour for the security of the state; they should not invite dangers recklessly, nor avoid them through timidity; they should show bravery against the enemy, not against their comrades, defend manfully the post assigned, and prefer a death of honour to a life of disgrace.

13. Those employed by the state in alien countries should be prudent and watchful, and proficient in discerning illusion from reality, and truth from fiction, they should be adherent to secrets, and tenacious in maintaining the interest of their country against any manner of dishonesty.

14. Those who care for the gathering and disbursement of the assets of the state ought to avoid all unnecessary severity, and not add any charge for their own gain, or from vexation or malignancy; they are not to keep any public money for their own use; and are to pay those to whom the state owes money without needless delay.

15. The duration of a special duty of a citizen is while they hold the office from which the duty arises; on leaving the office the duty of it expires. Similarly general duties last while they are citizens. They cease to be citizens if, with the express or tacit consent of the state, they come to reside in some other country: if in consequence of some crime, they are exiled and their right of citizenship is removed; or if having been overpowered by enemy force, are compelled to accede to the command of the conqueror.

Samuel Von Pufendorf, 'On the Duties of Citizens' [1682], in *De Officio Hominis et Civis Juxta Legem Naturalem Libri Duo by Samuel Von Pufendorf*, ed. Walther Schucking, *The Classics of International Law*, vol. 1: The Photographic Reproduction of the Edition of 1682 (New York: Oxford University Press, 1927), pp. 161–4.

5. When Virtue is Absent Avarice is Present

Charles de Secondat Montesquieu 1689–1755

There is no great share of probity necessary to support a monarchical or despotic government. The force of laws in one, and the prince's arm in the other, are sufficient to direct and maintain the whole. But in a popular state, one spring more is necessary, namely, *virtue* ...

The politic Greeks, who lived under a popular government, knew no other support than virtue. The modern inhabitants of that country are entirely taken up with manufacture, commerce, finances, opulence, and luxury.

When virtue is banished, ambition invades the minds of those who are disposed to receive it, and avarice possesses the whole community. The objects of their desires are changed; what they were fond of before has become indifferent; they were free while under the restraint of laws, but they would fain now be free to act against law; and as each citizen is like a slave who has run away from his master, that which was a maxim of equity he calls rigour; that which was a rule of action he styles constraint; and to precaution he gives the name of fear. Frugality, and not the thirst of gain, now passes for avarice. Formerly the wealth of individuals constituted the public treasure; but now this has become the patrimony of private persons. The members of the commonwealth riot on the public spoils, and its strength is only the power of a few, and the licence of many ...

In every government there are three sorts of power: the legislative; the executive in respect to things dependent on the law of nations; and the executive in regard to matters that depend on the civil law.

By virtue of the first, the prince or magistrate enacts temporary or perpetual laws, and amends or abrogates those that have been already enacted. By the second, he makes peace or war, sends or receives embassies, establishes the public security, and provides against invasions. By the third, he punishes criminals, or determines the disputes that arise between individuals. The latter we shall call the judiciary power, and the other simply the executive power of the state.

The political liberty of the subject is a tranquillity of mind arising from the opinion each person has of his safety. In order to have this liberty, it is requisite the government be so constituted as one man need not be afraid of another.

When the legislative and executive powers are united in the same person, or in the same body of magistrates, there can be no liberty; because apprehensions may arise, lest the same monarch or senate should enact tyrannical laws, to execute them in a tyrannical manner.

Again, there is no liberty, if the judiciary power be not separated from the legislative and executive. Were it joined with the legislative, the life and liberty of the subject would be exposed to arbitrary control; for the judge would be then the legislator. Were it joined to the executive power, the judge might behave with violence and oppression.

There would be an end of everything, were the same man or the same body, whether of the nobles or of the people, to exercise those three powers, that of enacting laws, that of executing the public resolutions, and of trying the causes of individuals ...

In what a situation must the poor subject be in those republics! The same body of magistrates are possessed, as executors of the laws, of the whole power they have given themselves in quality of legislators. They may plunder the state by their general determinations; and as they have likewise the judiciary power in their hands, every private citizen may be ruined by their particular decisions ...

It is not sufficient to have treated of political liberty in relation to the constitution; we must examine it likewise in the relation it bears to the subject.

We have observed that in the former case it arises from a certain distribution of the three powers; but in the latter, we must consider it in another light. It consists in security, or in the opinion people have of their security.

The constitution may happen to be free, and the subject not. The subject may be free, and not the constitution. In those cases, the constitution will be free by right, and not in fact; the subject will be free in fact, and not by right.

It is the disposition only of the laws, and even of the fundamental laws, that constitutes liberty in relation to the constitution. But as it regards the subject: manners, customs, or received examples may give rise to it, and particular civil laws may encourage it, as we shall presently observe.

Further, as in most states liberty is more checked or depressed than their constitution requires, it is proper to treat of the particular laws that in each constitution are apt to assist or check the principle of liberty which each state is capable of receiving.

Philosophic liberty consists in the free exercise of the will; or at least, if we must speak agreeably to all systems, in an opinion that we have the free exercise of our will. Political liberty consists in security, or, at least, in the opinion that we enjoy security.

This security is never more dangerously attacked than in public or private accusations. It is, therefore, on the goodness of criminal laws that the liberty of the subject principally depends ...

When the subject has no fence to secure his innocence, he has none for his liberty ...

Liberty is in perfection when criminal laws derive each punishment from the particular nature of the crime. There are then no arbitrary decisions; the punishment does not flow from the capriciousness of the legislator, but from the very nature of the thing; and man uses no violence to man.

There are four sorts of crimes. Those of the first species are prejudicial to religion, the second to morals, the third to the public tranquillity, and the fourth to the security of the subject. The punishments inflicted for these crimes ought to proceed from the nature of each of these species ...

The punishments inflicted upon the latter crimes are such as are properly distinguished by that name. They are a kind of retaliation, by which the society refuses security to a member, who has actually or intentionally deprived another of his security. These punishments are derived from the nature of the thing, founded on reason, and drawn from the very source of good and evil. A man deserves death when he has violated the security of the subject so far as to deprive, or attempt to deprive, another man of his life. This punishment of death is the remedy, as it were, of a sick society. When there is a breach of security with regard to property, there may be some reasons for inflicting a capital punishment: but it would be much better, and perhaps more natural, that crimes committed against the security of property should be punished with the loss of property; and this ought, indeed, to be the case if men's fortunes were common or equal. But as those who have no property of their own are generally the readiest to attack that of others, it has been found necessary, instead of a pecuniary, to substitute a corporal, punishment.

All that I have here advanced is founded in nature, and extremely favourable to the liberty of the subject.

Charles de Secondat Montesquieu, 'The Spirit of the Laws' [1748], in *The Spirit of the Laws by M. de Secondat Baron de Montesquieu*, tr. T. Nugent, vol. I (London: George Bell and Sons, 1878), pp. 21–3, 162–5, 196–201.

6. To Form Citizens is Not the Work of a Day

Jean-Jacques Rousseau 1712–78

... the first rule of public economy is that the administration of justice should be conformable to the laws. It will even be enough to prevent the State from being ill governed, that the Legislator shall have provided, as he should, for every need of place, climate, soil, custom, neighbourhood, and all the rest of the relations peculiar to the people he had to institute. Not but what there still remains an infinity of details of administration and economy, which are left to the wisdom of the government: but there are two infallible rules for its good conduct on these occasions; one is, that the spirit of the law ought to decide in every particular case that could not be foreseen; the other is that the general will, the source and supplement of all laws, should be consulted wherever they fail ...

The second essential rule of public economy is no less important than the first. If you would have the general will accomplished, bring all the particular wills into conformity with it; in other words, as virtue is nothing more than this conformity of the particular wills with the general will, establish the reign of virtue.

If our politicians were less blinded by their ambition, they would see how impossible it is for any establishment whatever to act in the spirit of its institution, unless it is guided in accordance with the law of duty; they would feel that the greatest support of public authority lies in the hearts of the citizens, and that nothing can take the place of morality in the maintenance of government. It is not only upright men who know how to administer the laws; but at bottom only good men know how to obey them.

... when the citizens love their duty, and the guardians of the public authority sincerely apply themselves to the fostering of that love by their own example and assiduity, every difficulty vanishes; and government becomes so easy that it needs none of that art of darkness, whose blackness is its only mystery. Those enterprising spirits, so dangerous and so much admired, all those great ministers, whose glory is inseparable from the miseries of the people, are no longer regretted: public morality supplies what is wanting in the genius of the rulers; and the more virtue reigns, the less need there is for talent ...

It is not enough to say to the citizens, *be good*; they must be taught to be so; and even example, which is in this respect the first lesson, is not the sole means to be employed; patriotism is the most efficacious: for, as I have said already, every man is virtuous when his particular will is in all things conformable to the general will, and we voluntarily will what is willed by those whom we love. It appears that the feeling of humanity evaporates and grows feeble in embracing all mankind, and that we cannot be affected by the calamities of Tartary or Japan, in the same manner as we are by those of European nations. It is necessary in some degree to confine and limit our interest and compassion in order to make it active. Now, as this sentiment can be useful only to those with whom we have to live, it is proper that our humanity should confine itself to our fellow-citizens, and should receive a new force because we are in the habit of seeing them, and by reason of the common interest which unites them. It is certain that the greatest miracles of virtue have been produced by patriotism: this fine and lively feeling, which gives to the force of self-love all the beauty of virtue, lends it an energy which, without disfiguring it, makes it the most heroic of all passions ...

Do we wish men to be virtuous? Then let us begin by making them love their country: but how can they love it, if their country be nothing more to them than to strangers, and afford them nothing but what it can refuse nobody? It would be still worse, if they did not enjoy even the privilege of social security, and if their lives, liberties, and property lay at the mercy of persons in power, without their being permitted, or its being possible for them, to make an appeal to the laws. For in that case, being subjected to the duties of the state of civil society, without enjoying even the common privileges of the state of nature, and without being able to use their strength in their own defence, they would be in the worst condition in which freemen could possibly find themselves, and the word 'country' would mean for them something merely odious and ridiculous. It must not be imagined that a man can break or lose an arm, without the pain being conveyed to his head: nor it is any more credible that the general will should consent that any one member of the State, whoever he might be, should wound or destroy another, than it is that the fingers of a man in his senses should wilfully scratch his eyes out. The security of individuals is so intimately connected with the public confederation that, apart from the regard that must be paid to human weakness, that convention would in point of right be dissolved, if in the State a single citizen who might have been relieved were allowed to perish, or if one were wrongfully confined in prison, or if in one case an obviously unjust sentence were given. For the fundamental conventions being broken, it is impossible to conceive of any right or interest that could retain the people in the social union; unless they were restrained by force, which alone causes the dissolution of the state of civil society.

In fact, does not the undertaking entered into by the whole body of the nation bind it to provide for the security of the least of its members with as much care as for that of all the rest? ...

Show respect, therefore, to your fellow-citizens, and you will render yourselves worthy of respect; show respect to liberty, and your power will increase daily. Never exceed your rights, and they will soon become unlimited.

Let our country then show itself the common mother of her citizens; let the advantages they enjoy in their country endear it to them; let the government leave them enough share in the public administration to make them feel that they are at home; and let the laws be in their eyes only the guarantees of the common liberty. These rights, great as they are, belong to all men ...

I conclude this part of public economy where I ought to have begun it. There can be no patriotism without liberty, no liberty without virtue, no virtue without citizens; create citizens, and you have everything you need; without them, you will have nothing but debased slaves, from the rulers of the State downwards. To form citizens is not the work of a day; and in order to have men it is necessary to educate them when they are children. It will be said, perhaps, that whoever has men to govern, ought not to seek, beyond their nature, a perfection of which they are incapable; that he ought not to desire to destroy their passions; and that the execution of such an attempt is no more desirable than it is possible. I will agree, further, that a man without passions would certainly be a bad citizen; but it must be agreed also that, if men are not taught not to love some things, it is impossible to teach them to love one object more than another – to prefer that which is truly beautiful to that which is deformed. If, for example, they were early accustomed to regard their individuality only in its relation to the body of the State, and to be aware, so to speak, of their own existence merely as a part of that of the State, they might at length come to identify themselves in some degree with this greater whole, to feel themselves members of their country, and to love it with that exquisite feeling which no isolated person has save for himself; to lift up their spirits perpetually to this great object, and thus to transform into a sublime virtue that dangerous disposition which gives rise to all our vices. Not only does philosophy demonstrate the possibility of taking steps in these new directions; history furnishes us with a thousand striking examples. If they are so rare among us moderns, it is because nobody troubles himself whether citizens exist or not, and still less does anybody think of attending to the matter soon enough to make them. It is too late to change our natural inclinations, when they have taken their course, and egoism is confirmed by habit: and it is too late to lead us out of ourselves when once the human ego, concentrated in our hearts, has acquired that contemptible activity which absorbs all virtue and constitutes the life and being of little minds. How can patriotism germinate in the midst of so many other passions which smother it? And what can remain, for fellow-citizens, of a heart already divided between avarice, a mistress, and vanity?

From the first moment of life, men ought to begin learning to deserve to live; and, as at the instant of birth we partake of the rights of citizenship, that instant ought to be the beginning of the exercise of our duty. If there are laws for the age of maturity, there ought to be laws for infancy, teaching obedience to others: and as the reason of each man is not left to be the sole arbiter of his duties, government ought the less indiscriminately to abandon to the intelligence and prejudices of fathers the education of their children, as that education is of still greater importance to the State than to the fathers: for, according to the course of nature, the death of the father often deprives him of the final fruits of education; but his country sooner or later perceives its effects. Families dissolve, but the State remains ...

It is not enough to have citizens and to protect them, it is also necessary to consider their subsistence. Provision for the public wants is an obvious inference from the general will, and the third essential duty of government. This duty is not, we should feel, to fill the granaries of individuals and thereby to grant them a dispensation from labour, but to keep plenty so within their reach that labour is always necessary and never useless for its acquisition. It extends also to everything regarding the management of the exchequer, and the expenses of public administration. Having thus treated of general economy with reference to the government of persons, we must now consider it with reference to the administration of property.

This part presents no fewer difficulties to solve, and contradictions to remove, than the preceding. It is certain that the right of property is the most sacred of all the rights of citizenship, and even more important in some respects than liberty itself; either because it more nearly affects the preservation of life, or because, property being more easily usurped and more difficult to defend than life, the law ought to pay a greater attention to what is most easily taken away; or finally, because property is the true foundation of civil society, and the real guarantee of the undertakings of citizens: for if property were not answerable for personal actions, nothing would be easier than to evade duties and laugh at the laws. On the other hand, it is no less certain that the maintenance of the State and the government involves costs and outgoings; and as every one who agrees to the end must acquiesce in the means, it follows that the members of a society ought to contribute from their property to its support. Besides, it is difficult to secure the property of individuals on one side, without attacking it on another; and it is impossible that all the regulations which govern the order of succession, will, contracts, etc., should not lay individuals under some constraint as to the disposition of their goods, and should not consequently restrict the right of property.

But besides what I have said above of the agreement between the authority of law and the liberty of the citizen, there remains to be made, with respect to the disposition of goods, an important observation which removes many difficulties. As Pufendorf has shown, the right of property, by its very nature, does not extend beyond the life of the proprietor, and the moment a man is dead his goods cease to belong to him. Thus, to prescribe the conditions according to which he can dispose of them, is in reality less to alter his right as it appears, than to extend it in fact.

In general, although the institution of the laws which regulate the power of individuals in the disposition of their own goods belongs only to the Sovereign, the spirit of these laws, which the government ought to follow in their application, is that, from father to son, and from relation to relation, the goods of a family should go as little out of it and be as little alienated as possible. There is a sensible reason for this in favour of children, to whom the right of property would be quite useless, if the father left them nothing, and who besides, having often contributed by their labour to the acquisition of their father's wealth, are in their own right associates with him in his right of property. But another reason, more distant, though not less important, is that nothing is more fatal to morality and to the Republic than the continual shifting of rank and fortune among the citizens: such changes are both the proof and the source of a thousand disorders, and overturn and confound everything; for those who were brought up to one thing find themselves destined for another; and neither those who rise nor those who fall are able to assume the rules of conduct, or to possess themselves of the qualifications requisite for their new condition, still less to discharge the duties it entails ...

Jean-Jacques Rousseau, 'A Discourse on Political Economy' [1750], in *The Social Contract and Discourse*, tr. G.D.H. Cole (London: Dent, 1913), pp. 126–36, 138–40.

7. Citizens are Subject Only to Themselves

Jean-Jacques Rousseau 1712–78

... If then we discard from the social compact what is not of its essence, we shall find that it reduces itself to the following terms:

'*Each of us puts his person and all his power in common under the supreme direction of the general will, and, in our corporate capacity, we receive each member as an indivisible part of the whole.*'

At once, in place of the individual personality of each contracting party, this act of association creates a corporate and collective body, composed of as many members as the assembly contains voters, and receiving from this act its unity, its common identity, its life, and its will. This public person, so formed by the union of all other persons, formerly took the name of *city*, and now takes that of *Republic* or *body politic*; it is called by its members *State* when passive, *Sovereign* when active, and *Power* when compared with others like itself. Those who are associated in it take collectively the name of *people*, and severally are called *citizens*, as sharing in the sovereign authority, and *subjects*, as being under the laws of the State. But these terms are often confused and taken one for another: it is enough to know how to distinguish them when they are being used with precision ...

It is therefore essential, if the general will is to be able to make itself known, that there should be no partial society in the State and that each citizen should express only his own opinion: which was indeed the sublime and unique system established by the great Lycurgus. But if there are partial societies, it is best to have as many as possible and to prevent them from being unequal, as was done by Solon, Numa, and Servius. These precautions are the only ones that can guarantee that the general will shall be always enlightened, and that the people shall in no way deceive itself.

If the State is a moral person whose life is in the union of its members, and if the most important of its cares is the care for its own preservation, it must have a universal and compelling force, in order to move and dispose each part as may be most advantageous to the whole. As nature gives each man absolute power over all his members, the social compact gives the body politic absolute power over all its members also; and it is this power which, under the direction of the general will, bears, as I have said, the name of Sovereignty.

But, besides the public person, we have to consider the private persons composing it, whose life and liberty are naturally independent of it. We are bound then to distinguish clearly between the respective rights of the citizens and the Sovereign, and between the duties the former have to fulfil as subjects, and the natural rights they should enjoy as men.

Each man alienates, I admit, by the social compact, only such part of his powers, goods, and liberty as it is important for the community to control; but it must also be granted that the Sovereign is sole judge of what is important.

Every service a citizen can render the State he ought to render as soon as the Sovereign demands it; but the Sovereign, for its part, cannot impose upon its subjects any fetters that are useless to the community, nor can it even wish to do so; for no more by the law of reason than by the law of nature can anything occur without a cause.

The undertakings which bind us to the social body are obligatory only because they are mutual; and their nature is such that in fulfilling them we cannot work for others without working for ourselves. Why is it that the general will is always upright, and that all continually will the happiness of each one, unless it is because there is not a man who does not think of 'each' as meaning him, and consider himself in voting for all? This proves that equality of rights and the idea of justice which such equality creates originate in the preference each man gives to himself, and accordingly in the very nature of man. It proves that the general will, to be really such, must be general in its object as well as its essence; that it must both come from all and apply to all; and that it loses its natural rectitude when it is directed to some particular and determinate object, because in such a case we are judging of something foreign to us, and have no true principle of equity to guide us.

Indeed, as soon as a question of particular fact or right arises on a point not previously regulated by a general convention, the matter becomes contentious. It is a case in which the individuals concerned are one party, and the public the other, but in which I can see neither the law that ought to be followed nor the judge who ought to give the decision. In such a case, it would be absurd to propose to refer the question to an express decision of the general will, which can be only the conclusion reached by one of the parties and in consequence will be, for the other party, merely an external and particular will, inclined on this occasion to injustice and subject to error. Thus, just as a particular will cannot stand for the general will, the general will, in turn, changes its nature, when its object is particular, and, as general, cannot pronounce on a man or a fact. When, for instance, the people of Athens nominated or displaced its rulers, decreed honours to one, and imposed penalties on another, and, by a multitude of particular decrees, exercised all the functions of government indiscriminately, it had in such cases no longer a general will in the strict sense; it was acting no longer as Sovereign, but as magistrate. This will seem contrary to current views; but I must be given time to expound my own.

It should be seen from the foregoing that what makes the will general is less the number of voters than the common interest uniting them; for, under this system, each necessarily submits to the conditions he imposes on others: and this admirable agreement between interest and justice gives to the common deliberations an equitable character which at once vanishes when any particular question is discussed, in the absence of a common interest to unite and identify the ruling of the judge with that of the party.

From whatever side we approach our principle, we reach the same conclusion, that the social compact sets up among the citizens an equality of such a kind, that they all bind themselves to observe the same conditions and should therefore all enjoy the same rights. Thus, from the very nature of the compact, every act of Sovereignty, i.e. every authentic act of the general will, binds or favours all the citizens equally; so that the Sovereign recognizes only the body of the nation, and draws no distinctions between those of whom it is made up. What, then, strictly speaking, is an act of Sovereignty? It is not a convention between a superior and an inferior, but a convention between the body and each of its members. It is legitimate, because based on the social contract, and equitable, because common to all; useful, because it can have no other object than the general good, and stable, because guaranteed by the public force and the supreme power. So long as the subjects have to submit only to conventions of this sort, they obey no one but their own will.

Jean-Jacques Rousseau, 'The Social Contract' in *The Social Contract and Discourses*, tr. G.D.H. Cole (London: Dent, 1913), pp. 175, 185–8.

8. Active and Passive Citizens

Immanuel Kant 1724–1804

A State (*civitas*) is the union of a number of men under principles of right. These principles are to be regarded as necessary a priori and follow from the general concepts of external right rather than being established merely by statute. The Form of the State is involved in the Idea of the State regarded as it ought to be in accordance with pure principles of right and this ideal provides a norm for every real instance where men unite in a commonwealth.

Every State includes within itself three powers, the universal united

Will of the people is incorporated in a political triad composed of three persons; the legislative power, the executive power, and the judicial power. The sovereign authority rests in the person of the legislator. Executive authority rests in the person of the ruler acting in conformity to law, and the judicial power of assigning to everyone what is his by law, resides in the person of the judge ...

The legislative authority viewed from the point of view of its rational principle can belong only to the united will of the people. As all right precedes from this authority it is necessary that its laws should not be unjust to anyone. If any one individual determines anything in the State in contradistinction to another, it is always possible that he may perpetrate a wrong on that other. However this is never possible when all determine and decree what is to be a law to themselves, 'Volenti non fit injuria' ['He who agrees cannot be injured']. Hence it is only the united and combined will of everyone, where each decides the same for all, and all decide for each, that ought to have the power to legislate in the State.

The members of a civil society, who unite for the purpose of enacting laws and which constitute a state, are designated as citizens. There are three rightful attributes inseparable from the nature of a citizen. First, the lawful freedom to obey only those laws to which he has consented. Second, the civil equality of being able to decline recognition of anyone as being superior to himself; except another whom he has as much of a moral entitlement to bind in law as the other has to bind him in law. Third, the attribute of civil independence requires him to owe his existence, and sustenance, to his own rights and powers as a member of the commonwealth rather than to the arbitrary will of another. His own civil personality, therefore, may not be represented by another where matters of justice and rights are concerned ...

The capacity to vote is a prerequisite of being a citizen. To have such a capacity presupposes that a person is politically independent not just as an incidental part of the commonwealth, but also a member of it, that is, one who, together with others, acts in accordance with his own will, as an active part of the commonwealth. This last qualification leads to the distinction between an active and a passive citizen, although the latter conception appears to contradict the definition of the citizen as such. The following examples may serve to remove this difficulty. The apprentice of a merchant or artisan; a servant who is not in the service of the State; a minor (naturaliter vel civiliter); all women, and, generally everyone who must depend for his support, not on his own industry, but on arrangements made by others (the state excepted) lack civil personality, and their existence is only, as it were, incidentally included in the State. The woodcutter whom I employ on my estate; the smith in India who carries his hammer, anvil and bellows in to the houses where he is engaged to work in iron, as distinguished from the European carpenter or smith who can offer the independent products of his labour as goods for public sale; the resident tutor as distinguished from the schoolmaster; the ploughman as distinguished from the farmer and such like, illustrate the distinction in question. In all these cases the former members of the contrast are distinguished from the latter by being mere subsidiaries of the commonwealth and not active independent members of it, because they are of necessity commanded by and protected by others and consequently possess no political self-sufficiency in themselves. Such dependence on the Will of others and the consequent inequality are, however, not incompatible with the freedom and equality of the individuals as Men helping to constitute the people. It is rather the case that, only by conforming to these conditions can a people become a State and enter into a Civil Constitution. But under the constitution, not everyone is equally qualified to have voting rights, that is, to be a citizen rather than as passive subjects under its protection. Although they are entitled to demand to be treated by all the other citizens according to laws of natural freedom and equality, as passive parts of the State, it does not follow that they ought themselves to have the right to deal with the State as active members of it, to reorganise it, or take action by way of introducing laws. All they have a right in their circumstances to claim, may be no more than that whatever be the mode in which the positive laws are enacted, these laws must not be contrary to the natural laws that demand the freedom of all the people and the equality that is conformable thereto; and it must therefore be made possible for them to raise themselves from this passive condition in the State, to the condition of active citizenship.

All these three Powers in the State are DIGNITIES; and as necessarily arising out of the Idea of the State and essential generally to the foundation of its Constitution, they are to be regarded as POLITICAL Dignities. They imply the relation between a universal SOVEREIGN as Head of the State – which according to the laws of freedom can be none other than the People itself united into a Nation – and the mass of the individuals of the Nation as SUBJECTS. The former member of the relation is the *ruling* Power, whose function it is to govern (*imperans*); the latter is the *ruled* Constituents of the State, whose function is to obey (*subditi*).

The act by which a People is represented as constituting itself into a State, is termed THE ORIGINAL CONTRACT. This is properly only an outward mode of representing the idea by which the rightfulness of the process of organising the Constitution, may be made conceivable. According to this Representation, all and each of the people give up their external freedom in order to receive it immediately again as Members of a Commonwealth, The Commonwealth is the people viewed as united altogether into a State ...

The three Powers in the State, as regards their relation to each other, are, therefore – (1) *co-ordinate* with one another as so many Moral Persons, and the one is thus the Complement of the other in the way of completing the Constitution of the State; (2) they are likewise *subordinate* to one another, so that the one cannot at the same time usurp the function of the other by whose side it moves, each having its own Principle, and maintaining its own authority in a particular person, but under the condition of the Will of a Superior; and, further, (3) by the *union* of both these relations, they assign distributively to every subject in the State his own Rights ...

... neither the Legislative Power nor the Executive Power ought to exercise the *judicial* Function, but only appoint Judges as Magistrates. It is the People who ought to judge themselves, through those of the Citizens who are elected by free Choice as the Representatives for this purpose, and even specially for every process or cause. For the judicial Sentence is a special act of public Distributive Justice performed by a Judge or Court as a constitutional Administrator of the Law, to a Subject as one of the People. Such an act is not invested inherently with the power to determine and assign to any one what is his. Every individual among the people being merely passive in this relation to the Supreme Power, either the Executive or the Legislative Authority might do him wrong in their determinations in cases of dispute regarding the property of individuals. It would not be the people themselves who thus determined, or who pronounced the judgments of 'guilty' or 'not guilty' regarding their fellow-citizens. For it is to the determination of this issue in a cause, that the Court has to apply the Law; and it is by means of the Executive Authority, that the Judge holds power to assign to every one his own. Hence it is only the *People* that properly can judge in a cause – although indirectly – by Representatives elected and deputed by themselves, as in a Jury ...

It is by the co-operation of these three Powers – the Legislative, the Executive, and the Judicial – that the State realises its *Autonomy*. This Autonomy consists in its organising, forming and maintaining itself in accordance with the Laws of Freedom. In their union the *Welfare* of the State is realised ... By this is not to be understood merely the individual *well-being* and *happiness* of the Citizens of the State; for – as Rousseau asserts – this End may perhaps be more agreeably and more desirably attained in the state of Nature, or even under a despotic Government. But the Welfare of the State as its own Highest Good, signifies that condition in which the greatest harmony is attained between its Constitution and the Principles of Right, – a condition of the State which

Reason by a Categorical Imperative makes it obligatory upon us to strive after.

Immanuel Kant, 'The Metaphysics of Morals, Part One: The Metaphysical Elements of Right' [1785], in Ernst Cassirer, *Kant's Werke*, vol. 7 Based on the translation by W.D. Hastie, *The Philosophy of Law*, sections 45–7 (Edinburgh: T. and T. Clark, 1887).

Part VI

A New World Order

1. From the Declaration of Independence, 1776

When in the course of human events, it becomes necessary for one people to dissolve the political bands which have connected them with another, and to assume among the powers of the earth, the separate and equal station to which the Laws of Nature and of Nature's God entitle them, a decent respect to the opinions of mankind requires that they should declare the causes which impel them to the separation.

We hold these truths to be self-evident, that all men are created equal, that they are endowed by their Creator with certain unalienable rights, that among these are life, liberty and the pursuit of happiness. That to secure these rights, governments are instituted among men, deriving their just powers from the consent of the governed. That whenever any form of government becomes destructive of these ends, it is the right of the people to alter or to abolish it, and to institute new government, laying its foundation on such principles and organizing its powers in such form, as to them shall seem most likely to effect their safety and happiness. Prudence, indeed, will dictate that governments long established should not be changed for light and transient causes; and accordingly all experience hath shown, that mankind are more disposed to suffer, while evils are sufferable, than to right themselves by abolishing the forms to which they are accustomed. But when a long train of abuses and usurpations, pursuing invariably the same object evinces a design to reduce them under absolute despotism, it is their right, it is their duty, to throw off such government, and to provide new guards for their future security. Such has been the patient sufferance of these Colonies; and such is now the necessity which constrains them to alter their former systems of government. The history of the present King of Great Britain is a history of repeated injuries and usurpations, all having in direct object the establishment of an absolute tyranny over these States. To prove this, let facts be submitted to a candid world.

He has refused his assent to laws, the most wholesome and necessary for the public good.

He has forbidden his Governors to pass laws of immediate and pressing importance, unless suspended in their operation till his assent should be obtained; and when so suspended, he has utterly neglected to attend to them.

He has refused to pass other laws for the accommodation of large districts of people, unless those people would relinquish the right of representation in the Legislature, a right inestimable to them and formidable to tyrants only.

He has called together legislative bodies at places unusual, uncomfortable, and distant from the depository of their public records, for the sole purpose of fatiguing them into compliance with his measures.

He has dissolved representative houses repeatedly, for opposing with manly firmness his invasions on the rights of the people.

He has refused for a long time, after such dissolutions, to cause others to be elected; whereby the legislative powers, incapable of annihilation, have returned to the people at large for their exercise; the State remaining in the meantime exposed to all the dangers of invasion from without and convulsions within.

He has endeavoured to prevent the population of these states; for that purpose obstructing the laws of naturalization of foreigners; refusing to pass others to encourage their migration hither, and raising the conditions of new appropriations of lands.

He has obstructed the administration of justice, by refusing his assent to laws for establishing judiciary powers.

He has made judges dependent on his will alone, for the tenure of their offices, and the amount and payment of their salaries.

He has erected a multitude of new offices, and sent hither swarms of officers to harass our people, and eat out their substance.

He has kept among us, in times of peace, standing armies without the consent of our legislatures.

He has affected to render the military independent of and superior to the civil power.

He has combined with others to subject us to a jurisdiction foreign to our constitution, and unacknowledged by our laws; giving his assent to their acts of pretended legislation:

For quartering large bodies of armed troops among us:

For protecting them, by a mock trial, from punishment for any murders which they should commit on the inhabitants of these States:

For cutting off our trade with all parts of the world:

For imposing taxes on us without our consent:

For depriving us in many cases, of the benefits of trial by jury:

For transporting us beyond seas to be tried for pretended offences:

For abolishing the free system of English laws in a neighbouring Province, establishing therein an arbitrary government, and enlarging its boundaries so as to render it at once an example and fit instrument for introducing the same absolute rule into these Colonies:

For taking away our Charters, abolishing our most valuable laws, and altering fundamentally the forms of our government:

For suspending our own Legislatures, and declaring themselves invested with power to legislate for us in all cases whatsoever.

He has abdicated government here, by declaring us out of his protection and waging war against us.

He has plundered our seas, ravaged our coasts, burnt our towns, and destroyed the lives of our people.

He is at this time transporting large armies of foreign mercenaries to complete the works of death, desolation and tyranny, already begun with circumstances of cruelty and perfidy scarcely paralleled in the most barbarous ages, and totally unworthy the head of a civilized nation.

He has constrained our fellow citizens taken captive on the high seas to bear arms against their country, to become the executioners of their friends and brethren, or to fall themselves by their hands.

He has excited domestic insurrections amongst us, and has endeavoured to bring on the inhabitants of our frontiers, the merciless Indian savages, whose known rule of warfare, is an undistinguished destruction of all ages, sexes, and conditions.

In every stage of these oppressions we have petitioned for redress in the most humble terms: our repeated petitions have been answered only by repeated injury. A prince whose character is thus marked by every act which may define a tyrant is unfit to be the ruler of a free people.

Nor have we been wanting in attention to our British brethren. We have warned them from time to time of attempts by their legislature to extend an unwarrantable jurisdiction over us. We have reminded them of the circumstances of our emigration and settlement here. We have appealed to their native justice and magnanimity, and we have conjured them by the ties of our common kindred to disavow these usurpations, which would inevitably interrupt our connections and correspondence. They too have been deaf to the voice of justice and of consanguinity. We must, therefore, acquiesce in the necessity, which denounces our separation, and hold them, as we hold the rest of mankind, enemies in war, in peace friends.

We, therefore, the Representatives of the United States of America, in General Congress assembled, appealing to the Supreme Judge of the world for the rectitude of our intentions, do, in the name, and by authority of the good people of these Colonies, solemnly publish and declare, That these United Colonies are, and of right ought to be Free and Independent States; that they are absolved from all allegiance to the British Crown, and that all political connection between them and the State of Great Britain, is and ought to be totally dissolved; and that as Free and Independent States, they have full power to levy war, conclude peace, contract alliances, establish commerce, and to do all other acts and things which Independent States may of right do. And for the support of this declaration, with a firm reliance on the protection of Divine Providence, we mutually pledge to each other our lives, our fortunes, and our sacred honor.

2. From the Constitution of the United States of America, 1787

Article 1

Sec. 2. The House of Representatives shall be composed of members chosen every second year by the people of the several States, and the electors in each State shall have the qualifications requisite for electors of the most numerous branch of the State legislature.

No person shall be a Representative who shall not have attained to the age of twenty-five years, and been seven years a citizen of the United States, and who shall not, when elected, be an inhabitant of that State in which he shall be chosen ...

Sec. 3. ... No person shall be a Senator who shall not have attained to the age of thirty years, and been nine years a citizen of the United States, and who shall not, when elected, be an inhabitant of that State for which he shall be chosen ...

Sec. 8. The Congress shall have power to ... establish an uniform rule of naturalization... throughout the United States ...

Article II

Sec. 1. No person except a natural-born citizen, or a citizen of the United States, at the time of the adoption of this Constitution, shall be eligible to the office of President; neither shall any person be eligible to that office who shall not have attained to the age of thirty-five years, and been fourteen years a resident within the United States.

Article IV

Sec. 2. The citizens of each State shall be entitled to all privileges and immunities of citizens in the several States ...

Article XIV (1868)

Sec. 1. All persons born or naturalized in the United States, and subject to the jurisdiction thereof, are citizens of the United States and of the State wherein they reside. No State shall make or enforce any law which shall abridge the privileges or immunities of citizens of the United States; nor shall any State deprive any person of life, liberty, or property, without due process of law; nor deny to any person within its jurisdiction the equal protection of the laws.

Sec. 2. Representatives shall be appointed among the several States according to their respective numbers, counting the whole number of persons in each State, excluding Indians not taxed. But when the right to vote at any election for the choice of electors for President and Vice-President of the United States, Representatives in Congress, the executive and judicial officers of a State, or the members of the legislature thereof, is denied to any of the male inhabitants of such State, being twenty-one years of age, and citizens of the United States, or in any way abridged, except for participation in rebellion, or other crime, the basis of representation therein shall be reduced in the proportion which the number of such male citizens shall bear to the whole number of male citizens twenty-one years of age in such State ...

3. From the Declaration of the Rights of Man and of Citizens, 1789

The representatives of the people of France, formed into a National Assembly, considering that ignorance, neglect, or contempt of human rights are the sole causes of public misfortunes and corruptions of government, have resolved to set forth in a solemn declaration these natural, imprescriptible, and unalienable rights; that, this declaration being constantly present to the minds of the members of the body social, they may be ever kept attentive to their rights and their duties; that the acts of the legislative and executive powers of government, being capable of being every moment compared with the end of political institutions, may be more respected; and also that the future claims of the citizens, being directed by simple and incontestable principles, may always tend to the maintenance of the constitution and the general happiness.

For these reasons the National Assembly does recognize and declare, in the presence of the Supreme Being, and with the hope of His blessing and favor, the following *sacred* rights of men and of citizens:

I. *Men are born, and always continue, free and equal in respect of their rights. Civil distinctions, therefore, can be founded only on public utility.*

II. *The end of all political associations is the preservation of the natural and imprescriptible rights of man; and these rights are liberty, property, security, and resistance of oppression.*

III. *The nation is essentially the source of all sovereignty; nor can any individual or any body of men be entitled to any authority which is not expressly derived from it.*

IV. Political liberty consists in the power of doing whatever does not injure another. The exercise of the natural rights of every man has no other limits than those which are necessary to secure to every *other* man the free exercise of the same rights, and these limits are determinable only by the law.

V. The law ought to prohibit only actions hurtful to society. What is not prohibited by the law should not be hindered; nor should anyone be compelled to that which the law does not require.

VI. The law is an expression of the will of the community. All citizens have a right to concur, either personally or by their representatives, in its formation. It should be the same to all, whether it protects or punishes; and *all being equal in its sight are equally eligible to all honors, places, and employments, according to their different abilities, without any other distinction than that created by their virtues and talents.*

VII. No man should be accused, arrested, or held in confinement, except in cases determined by the law and according to the forms which it has prescribed. All who promote, solicit, execute, or cause to be executed arbitrary orders ought to be punished, and every citizen called upon or apprehended by virtue of the law ought immediately to obey and renders himself culpable by resistance.

VIII. The law ought to impose no other penalties but such as are absolutely and evidently necessary, and no one ought to be punished but in virtue of a law promulgated before the offense and legally applied.

IX. Every man being presumed innocent till he has been convicted, whenever his detention becomes indispensable, all rigor to him – more than is necessary to secure his person – ought to be provided against by the law.

X. No man ought to be molested on account of his opinions, not even on account of his *religious* opinions, provided his avowal of them does not disturb the public order established by the law.

XI. The unrestrained communication of thoughts and opinions being one of the most precious rights of man, every citizen may speak, write, and publish freely, provided he is responsible for the abuse of this liberty in cases determined by the law.

XII. A public force being necessary to give security to the rights of men and of citizens, that force is instituted for the benefit of the community, and not for the particular benefit of the persons with whom it is entrusted.

XIII. A common contribution being necessary for the support of the public force and for defraying the other expenses of the government, it ought to be divided equally among the members of the community, according to their abilities.

XIV. Every citizen has a right, either by himself or his representative, to a free voice in determining the necessity of public contributions, the appropriation of them, and their amount, mode of assessment, and duration.

XV. Every community has a right to demand of all its agents an account of their conduct.

XVI. Every community in which a separation of powers and a security of rights is not provided for wants a constitution.

XVII. The rights to property being inviolable and sacred, no one ought to be deprived of it, except in cases of evident public necessity, legally ascertained, and on condition of a previous just indemnity.

'Declaration of the Rights of Man and of Citizens', reprinted in Thomas Paine, *The Rights of Man* [1791-2], in Hypatia B. Bonner (London: Watts and Co, 1937).

4. And Why Should Citizens Not Aspire to Public Offices?

Anna Laetitia Aikin Barbauld 1743-1825

We could wish to be considered as children of the State, though we are not so of the Church. She must excuse us if we look upon the alliance between her and the State as an ill-sorted union, and herself as a mother-in-law who, with the too frequent arts of that relation, is ever endeavouring to prejudice the State, the common father of us all, against a part of his offspring, for the sake of appropriating a larger portion to her own children. We claim no share in the dowry of her who is not our mother, but we may be pardoned for thinking it hard to be deprived of the inheritance of our father.

But it is objected to us that we have sinned in the manner of making our request, we have brought it forward as a claim instead of asking it as a favour. We should have sued, and crept, and humbled ourselves. Our preachers and our writers should not have dared to express the warm glow of honest sentiment, or, even in a foreign country glance at the downfall of a haughty aristocracy. As we were suppliants, we should have behaved like suppliants, and then perhaps – No, Gentlemen, we wish to have it understood, that we *do* claim it as a right. It loses otherwise half its value.

We claim it as men, we claim it as citizens, we claim it as good subjects. We are not conscious of having brought the disqualification upon ourselves by a failure in any of these characters.

But this it is again imputed to us is no contest for religious liberty, but a contest for power, and place, and influence. We want civil offices – And why should citizens *not* aspire to civil offices? Why should not the fair field of generous competition be freely opened to every one? – A contention for power – It is not a contention for power between Churchmen and

Dissenters, nor is it as Dissenters we wish to enter the lists; we wish to bury every name of distinction in the common appellation of Citizen. We wish not the name of Dissenter to be pronounced, except in our theological researches and religious assemblies. It is you, who by considering us as Aliens, make us so. It is you who force us to make our dissent a prominent feature in our character. It is you who give relief, and cause to come out upon the canvas what we modestly wished to have shaded over, and thrown into the background. If we are a party, remember it is you who force us to be so.

Anna Laetitia Aikin Barbauld, 'An Address to the Opposers of the Repeal of the Corporation and Test Acts'. Dissenter Papers (Aikin), London, 1790. British Museum 4106 f. 11.

5. Against the Poll Tax

Maximilien Marie Isidore de Robespierre 1758–94

Why are we gathered in this legislative assembly? Doubtless to restore to the French nation the exercise of imprescriptible rights that belong to every citizen. This is the main purpose of every political constitution. If it fulfills this obligation, it is just and free; if it fails to do so, it is nothing but a conspiracy against mankind.

You recognized this truth yourselves, and in a striking manner, when you decided, before beginning your great work, that a solemn declaration must be made of the sacred rights that serve as the immutable foundations on which it rests.

All men are born and remain free, and are equal at law.

Sovereignty derives from the nation as a whole.

The law is the expression of the general will. All citizens have the right to contribute to its making, either directly by themselves or through their freely elected representatives.

All citizens are admissible to every public office, and no distinction is made between them except in respect of their virtues and talents.

These are the principles that you have enshrined. It will now be readily seen which are the measures that I wish to combat; it is enough to test them against these immutable laws of human society.

1. Can the law be termed an expression of the general will when the greater number of those for whom it is made can have no hand in its making? No ...

2. Can men be said to enjoy equal rights when some are endowed with the exclusive right to be elected members of the legislative body or of

other public institutions, others merely with that of electing them, while the rest are deprived of all these rights at once? No ...

3. Are men admissible to all public posts, and is no distinction made except such as derive from their virtues and talents, when an inability to pay the required tax excludes them from every public office regardless of the virtues and talents that they may possess? No ...

4. And again, is the nation sovereign when the greater part of the persons composing it is deprived of the political rights from which sovereignty derives its essence? No ...

All men *born* and *domiciled* in France are members of the body politic termed the French nation; that is to say, they are French citizens. They are so by the nature of things and by the first principle of the law of nations. The rights attaching to this title do not depend on the fortune that each man possesses, nor on the amount of tax for which he is assessed, because it is not taxes that make us citizens: citizenship merely obliges a man to contribute to public expenditure in proportion to his means. You may give the citizens new laws, but you may not deprive them of their citizenship.

The upholders of the system that I am denouncing have themselves realized this truth; for, not daring to challenge the title of citizen in those whom they condemn to political disinheritance, they have confined themselves to destroying the principle of equality inherent in that title by drawing a distinction between active and passive citizens. Trusting in the ease with which men may be governed by words, they have sought to lead us off the scent by using this new expression as a cover for the most flagrant violation of the rights of man.

But who can be so stupid as not to perceive that such a phrase can neither invalidate the principle nor solve the problem? For, in the idiom of these subtle politicians, it is exactly the same thing to declare that certain citizens shall not be active as to say that they shall no longer exercise the rights attaching to the title of citizen. Well, I shall ask them once more by what right they may thus strike their fellow citizens and constitutents with paralysis and reduce them to inactivity; and I shall not cease protesting against this barbaric and insidious phrase which, if we do not hasten to efface it, will disgrace our language and our code of laws, so that the word 'liberty' itself may not become meaningless and laughable...

Have 26 million men entrusted you with the fearful charge of safeguarding their destiny in order that you may lightheartedly leave in this constitution fundamental vices that undermine the foundations of the social order? Perhaps you will say that the reform of a great number of abuses and the enactment of several useful laws are so many concessions to the people that dispense you from the obligation of doing more for them? No; all the good that you have done was a duty rigorously imposed.

To fail to do the good that you still have to do would be a distortion of justice; the evil that would result would be an act of treason against the nation and humanity. And more: if you do not do everything for liberty, you will have done nothing. There are not two ways of being free: one must be so entirely or one becomes once more a slave. Leave one solitary resource to despotism, and you will soon restore its power. Aye, already it seeks to seduce and to enthrall you; give an inch and it will hold you fully in its sway. O you who glory in having lent your names to a great change and are not too much concerned if it is sufficient to assure the happiness of mankind, do not be deceived: the chorus of praise that astonishment and shallow thinking have provoked will soon die away; and posterity, comparing the greatness of your obligations and the immensity of your resources with the fundamental vices of your work will say of you with indignation: 'They could have made men free and happy, but they did not wish to. They were unworthy of the task.'

But, you will say, shall the people, those who have nothing to lose, have the same rights of citizenship as we? Those who have nothing to lose! How false and unjust such language, begotten of delirious pride, appears in the sight of truth! ...

But what is, after all, the rare merit in paying a silver mark or such other tax on which you make such exalted privileges dependent? If you make a larger contribution to the public treasury than I, is it not because society has favored you with greater pecuniary advantages? And, if we wish to press the point further, what is the source of that extreme inequality of fortunes that concentrates all wealth in the hands of a few? Is it not the result of bad laws, of bad government and of all the vices of corrupted societies? Now, why should those who are the victims of these abuses be doubly punished for their misfortune by the loss of their dignity as citizens? I do not dispute your right to enjoy the unequal portion that you have received, since this inequality is a necessary or an incurable evil; but do not take from me, at least, the imprescriptible rights of which no manmade law is entitled to deprive me. Permit me even at times to be proud of an honorable poverty, and do not seek to humiliate me by arrogantly presuming to monopolize the title of sovereign while leaving me none other than that of subject.

But the people, you say, are prone to be corrupted!

... in spite of all your prejudice in favor of such virtues as come with wealth, I venture to believe that you will find as many among the poorest citizens as among the wealthiest! Do you honestly believe that a hard, laborious life engenders as many vices as one of comfort, luxury and ambition? And have you less faith in the probity of our artisans and peasants, who, according to your formula, will hardly ever be active citizens, as you have in that of tax-farmers, courtiers, and those whom you call great lords, who, following the same formula, would be so six hundred times over? Once and for all, I wish to avenge those whom you call the *people* for these sacrilegious slanders ...

The people demands only what is necessary, it merely wants justice and tranquillity: the rich lay claim to everything, they invade all others' rights and aim at universal domination. Social abuses are the handiwork and province of the rich, they are the scourge of the people. The interest of the people is the general interest, that of the rich is a particular interest; and yet you wish to give the people no voice in government and make the rich all-powerful! ...

Up to now, I have adopted the language of those who seem to mean by the word 'people' a class of men set aside from their fellows and to whom they attach a certain label of contempt or inferiority. It is now time that I express myself more precisely, in recalling that the system we condemn disfranchises nine-tenths of the nation and that it even excludes from the lists of those it terms active citizens vast numbers of men who, even in the bad old days of pride and prejudice, were honored and distinguished for their education, their industry, even for their fortunes ...

In short, what is the worth of my much vaunted right to belong to the sovereign body if the assessor of taxes has the power to deprive me of it by reducing my contribution by a cent and if it is subject at once to the caprice of man and the inconsistency of fortune?

Maximilien Marie Isidore de Robespierre, 'On the Right to Vote' [1791], in George Rudé (ed.), *Robespierre* Great Lives Observed series (Englewood Cliffs, NJ: Prentice Hall, 1967), pp. 14–22.

6. The Restraints on Men are among Their Rights

Edmund Burke 1729–97

... Far am I from denying in theory; full as far is my heart from withholding in practice (if I were of power to give or to withhold) the real rights of men. In denying their false claims of right, I do not mean to injure those which are real, and are such as their pretended rights would totally destroy. If civil society be made for the advantage of man, all the advantages for which it is made become his right. It is an institution of beneficence; and law itself is only beneficence acting by a rule. Men have a right to live by that rule; they have a right to justice; as between their fellows, whether their fellows are in politic function or in ordinary occupation. They have a right to the fruits of their industry; and to the means of making their industry fruitful. They have a right to the acquisitions of their parents; to the nourishment and improvement of their offspring; to instruction in life, and to consolation in death. Whatever each man can separately do, without trespassing upon others, he has a right to do for himself; and he has a right to a fair portion of all which society, with all its combinations of skill and force, can do in his favour. In this partnership all men have equal rights: but not to equal things. He that has but five shillings in the partnership, has as good a right to it, as he that has five hundred pounds has to his larger proportion. But he has not a right to an equal dividend in the product of the joint stock; and as to the share of power, authority, and direction which each individual ought to have in the management of the state, that I must deny to be amongst the direct original rights of man in civil society; for I have in my contemplation the civil social man, and no other. It is a thing to be settled by convention.

If civil society be the offspring of convention, that convention must be its law. That convention must limit and modify all the descriptions of constitution which are formed under it. Every sort of legislative judicial, or executory power are its creatures. They can have no being in any other state of things; and how can any man claim, under the conventions of civil society, rights which do not so much as suppose its existence? Rights which are absolutely repugnant to it? One of the first motives to civil society, and which becomes one of its fundamental rules, is, *that no man should be judge in his own cause.* By this each person has at once divested himself of the first fundamental right of uncovenanted man, that is, to judge for himself, and to assert his own cause. He abdicates all right to be his own governor. He inclusively, in a great measure, abandons the right of self defence, the first law of nature. Men cannot enjoy the rights of an uncivil and of a civil state together. That he may obtain justice he gives up his right of determining what it is in points the most essential to him. That he may secure some liberty, he makes a surrender in trust of the whole of it.

Government is not made in virtue of natural rights, which may and do exist in total independence of it; and exist in much greater clearness, and in a much greater degree of abstract perfection: but their abstract perfection is their practical defect. By having a right to every thing they want every thing. Government is a contrivance of human wisdom to provide for human *wants.* Men have a right that these wants should be provided for by this wisdom. Among these wants is to be reckoned the want, out of civil society, of a sufficient restraint upon their passions. Society requires not only that the passions of individuals should be subjected, but that even in the mass and body as well as in the individuals, the inclinations of men should frequently be thwarted, their will controlled, and their passions brought into subjection. This can only be done *by a power out of themselves*; and not, in the exercise of its function, subject to that will and to those passions which it is its office to bridle and subdue. In this sense the restraints on men, as well as their liberties, are to be reckoned among their rights ...

I do not know under what description to class the present ruling authority in France. It affects to be a pure democracy, though I think it in a direct train of becoming shortly a mischievous and ignoble oligarchy ...

I believe the present French power is the very first body of citizens, who, having obtained full authority to do with their country what they pleased, have chosen to dissever it in this barbarous manner.

It is impossible not to observe, that in the spirit of this geometrical distribution, and arithmetical arrangement, these pretended citizens treat France exactly like a country of conquest. Acting as conquerors, they have imitated the policy of the harshest of that harsh race. The policy of such barbarous victors, who contemn a subdued people, and insult their feelings, has ever been, as much as in them lay, to destroy all vestiges of the antient country, in religion, in polity, in laws, and in manners; to confound all territorial limits; to produce a general poverty; to put up their properties to auction; to crush their princes, nobles, and pontiffs; to lay low every thing which had lifted its head above the level, or which could serve to combine or rally, in their distresses, the disbanded people, under the standard of old opinion. They have made France free in the manner in which those sincere friends to the rights of mankind, the Romans, freed Greece, Macedon, and other nations. They destroyed the bonds of their union, under colour of providing for the independence of each of their cities ...

Edmund Burke, *Reflections on the Revolution in France* [1790] (Harmondsworth: Penguin, 1967), pp. 113–15.

7. Obedience is to Laws Not Men

Thomas Paine 1737–1809

When we survey the wretched condition of man, under the monarchical and hereditary systems of government, dragged from his home by one power, or driven by another, and impoverished by taxes more than by enemies, it becomes evident that those systems are bad, and that a general revolution in the principle and construction of governments is necessary.

What is government more than the management of the affairs of a nation? It is not, and from its nature cannot be, the property of any particular man or family, but of the whole community, at whose expence it is supported; and though by force and contrivance it has been usurped into an inheritance, the usurpation cannot alter the right of things. Sovereignty, as a matter of right, appertains to the nation only, and not to any individual; and a nation has at all times an inherent, indefeasible right to abolish any form of government it finds inconvenient, and to establish such as accords with its interest, disposition, and happiness. The romantic and barbarous distinction of men into Kings and subjects, though it may suit the conditions of courtiers, cannot that of citizens; and is exploded by the principle upon which governments are now founded. Every citizen is a member of the sovereignty, and, as such, can acknowledge no personal subjection: and his obedience can be only to the laws.

When men think of what government is, they must necessarily suppose it to possess a knowledge of all the objects and matters upon which its authority is to be exercised. In this view of government, the republican system, as established by America and France, operates to embrace the whole of a nation; and the knowledge necessary to the interest of all the parts, is to be found in the centre, which the parts by representation form; but the old governments are on a construction that excludes knowledge as well as happiness; government by monks, who knew nothing of the world beyond the walls of a convent, is as consistent as government by kings.

What were formerly called revolutions, were little more than a change of persons, or an alteration of local circumstances. They rose and fell like things of course, and had nothing in their existence or their fate that could influence beyond the spot that produced them. But what we now see in the world, from the revolutions of America and France, are a renovation of the natural orders of things, a system of principles as universal as truth and the existence of man, and combining moral with political happiness and national prosperity.

I. *Men are born, and always continue, free and equal in respect of their rights. Civil distinctions, therefore, can be founded only on public utility.*

II. *The end of all political associations is the preservation of the natural and imprescriptible rights of man; and these rights are liberty, property, security, and resistance of oppression.*

III. *The nation is essentially the source of all sovereignty; nor can ANY INDIVIDUAL, or ANY BODY OF MEN, be entitled to any authority which is not expressly derived from it.*

In these principles there is nothing to throw a nation into confusion by inflaming ambition. They are calculated to call forth wisdom and abilities, and to exercise them for the public good, and not for the emolument or aggrandisement of particular descriptions of men or families. Monarchical sovereignty, the enemy of mankind, and the source of misery, is abolished; and the sovereignty itself is restored to its natural and original place, the nation ...

Thomas Paine, *Rights of Man; Being an Answer to Mr. Burke's Attack on the French Revolution* [1791–2], ed. Hypatia B. Bonner (London: Watts and Co, 1937), pp. 54–5, 110–17.

8. Citizens Have a Duty to Keep a Watchful Eye on Government

London Corresponding Society

Man as an individual is entitled to liberty, it is his Birth-right.

As a member of society the preservation of that liberty becomes his indispensable duty.

When he associated he gave up certain rights, in order to secure the possession of the remainder;

But, he voluntarily yielded up only as much as was necessary for the common good:

He still preserved a right of sharing the government of his country; – without it no man can, with truth call himself *free*.

Fraud or force, sanctioned by custom, with-holds the right from (by far) the greater number of the inhabitants of this country.

The few with whom the right of election and representation remains abuse it, and the strong temptations held out to electors, sufficiently prove that the representatives of this country seldom procure a seat in parliament from the unbought suffrages of a free People.

The nation, at length, perceives it, and testifies an ardent desire of remedying the evil.

The only difficulty then, at present, is, the ascertaining the true method of proceeding.

To this end, different, and numerous Societies have been formed in different parts of the nation.

Several likewise have arisen in the Metropolis, and among them, (though as yet in its infant state), the Corresponding Society, with modesty intrudes itself and opinions, on the attention of the public in the following resolutions:

Resolved, – That every individual has a right to share in the government of that society of which he is a member – unless incapacitated.

Resolved, – That nothing but non-age, privation of reason, or an offence against the general rules of society can incapacitate him.

Resolved, – That it is no less the *right* than the *duty* of every Citizen, to keep a watchful eye on the government of his country; that the laws, by being multiplied, do not degenerate into *oppression*, and that those who are entrusted with the government, do not substitute private interest for public advantage.

Resolved, – That the people of Great Britain are not effectually represented in Parliament.

Resolved, – That in consequence of a partial, unequal, and therefore inadequate representation, together with the corrupt method in which representatives are elected; oppressive taxes, unjust laws, restrictions of liberty, and wasting the public money have ensued.

Resolved, – That the only remedy for those evils is a fair, equal and impartial representation of the People in Parliament.

Resolved, – That a fair, equal, and impartial representation of the People in Parliament can never take place until all partial privileges are abolished.

Resolved, – That this Society to express their *abhorrence* of tumults and violence, and that, as they aim at reform, not anarchy, but reason, firmness, and unanimity, are the only arms they themselves will employ, or persuade their fellow Citizens to exert against the Abuse of Power.

'Resolutions in the Minute Book of the London Corresponding Society', 2 April 1792. Place Papers. British Museum MSS 27812.

9. A Republic Can Control Factions

James Madison 1751–1836

To the People of the State of New York: Among the numerous advantages promised by a well constructed Union, none deserves to be more accurately developed than its tendency to break and control the violence of faction ...

The valuable improvements made by the American constitutions on the popular models, both ancient and modern, cannot certainly be too much admired; but it would be an unwarrantable partiality, to contend that they have as effectually obviated the danger on this side, as was wished and expected. Complaints are everywhere heard from our most considerate and virtuous citizens, equally the friends of public and private faith, and of public and personal liberty, that our governments are too unstable, that the public good is disregarded in the conflicts of rival parties, and that measures are too often decided, not according to the rules of justice and the rights of the minor party, but by the superior force of an interested and overbearing majority ...

By a faction, I understand a number of citizens, whether amounting to a majority or minority of the whole, who are united and actuated by some common impulse of passion, or of interest, adverse to the rights of other citizens, or to the permanent and aggregate interests of the community.

There are two methods of curing the mischiefs of faction: the one, by removing its causes; the other, by controlling its effects.

There are again two methods of removing the causes of faction: the one, by destroying the liberty which is essential to its existence; the other, by giving to every citizen the same opinions, the same passions, and the same interests.

It could never be more truly said than of the first remedy, that it was worse than the disease. Liberty is to faction what air is to fire, an aliment without which it instantly expires. But it could not be less folly to abolish liberty, which is essential to political life, because it nourishes faction, than it would be to wish the annihilation of air, which is essential to animal life, because it imparts to fire its destructive agency.

The second expedient is as impracticable as the first would be unwise. As long as the reason of man continues fallible, and he is at liberty to exercise it, different opinions will be formed ...

The latent causes of faction are thus sown in the nature of man; and we see them everywhere brought into different degrees of activity, according to the different circumstances of civil society. A zeal for different opinions concerning religion, concerning government, and many other points, as well of speculation as of practice; an attachment to different leaders ambitiously contending for pre-eminence and power; or to persons of other descriptions whose fortunes have been interesting to the human passions, have, in turn, divided mankind into parties, inflamed them with mutual animosity, and rendered them much more disposed to vex and oppress each other than to co-operate for their common good. So strong is this propensity of mankind to fall into mutual animosities, that where no substantial occasion presents itself, the most frivolous and fanciful distinctions have been sufficient to kindle their unfriendly passions and excite their most violent conflicts. But the most common and durable source of factions has been the various and unequal distribution of property ...

The inference to which we are brought is, that the *causes* of faction cannot be removed, and that relief is only to be sought in the means of controlling its *effects*.

If a faction consists of less than a majority, relief is supplied by the republican principle, which enables the majority to defeat its sinister view by regular vote. It may clog the administration, it may convulse the society; but it will be unable to execute and mask its violence under the forms of the Constitution. When a majority is included in a faction, the form of popular government, on the other hand, enables it to sacrifice to its ruling passion or interest both the public good and the rights of other citizens. To secure the public good and private rights against the danger of such a faction, and at the same time to preserve the spirit and the form of popular government, is then the great object to which our inquiries are directed ...

From this view of the subject it may be concluded that a pure democracy, by which I mean a society consisting of a small number of citizens, who assemble and administer the government in person, can admit of no cure for the mischiefs of faction. A common passion or interest will, in almost every case, be felt by a majority of the whole; a communication and concert result from the form of government itself; and there is nothing to check the inducements to sacrifice the weaker party or an obnoxious individual. Hence it is that such democracies have ever been spectacles of turbulence and contention; have ever been found incompatible with personal security or the rights of property; and have in general been as short in their lives as they have been violent in their deaths. Theoretic politicians, who have patronized this species of government, have erroneously supposed that by reducing mankind to a perfect equality in their political rights, they would, at the same time, be perfectly equalized and assimilated in their possessions, their opinions, and their passions.

A republic, by which I mean a government in which the scheme of representation takes place, opens a different prospect, and promises the cure for which we are seeking. Let me examine the points in which it varies from pure democracy, and we shall comprehend both the nature of the cure and the efficacy which it must derive from the Union.

The two great points of difference between a democracy and a republic are: first, the delegation of the government, in the latter, to a small number of citizens, elected by the rest; secondly, the greater number of citizens, and greater sphere of country, over which the latter may be extended.

The effect of the first difference is, on the one hand, to refine and enlarge the public views, by passing them through the medium of a chosen body of citizens, whose wisdom may best discern the true interest of their country, and whose patriotism and love of justice will be least likely to sacrifice it to temporary or partial consideration. Under such a regulation, it may well happen that the public voice, pronounced by the representatives of the people, will be more consonant to the public good than if pronounced by the people themselves, convened for the purpose. On the other hand, the effect may be inverted. Men of factious tempers, of local prejudices, or of sinister designs, may, by intrigue, by corruption, or by other means, first obtain the suffrages, and then betray the interests, of the people ...

The other point of difference is, the greater number of citizens and extent of territory which may be brought within the compass of republican than of democratic government; and it is this circumstance principally which renders factious combinations less to be dreaded in the former than in the latter. The smaller the society, the fewer probably will be the distinct parties and interests composing it; the fewer the distinct parties and interests, the more frequently will a majority be found of the same party;

and the smaller the number of individuals composing a majority, and the smaller the compass within which they are placed, the more easily will they concert and execute their plans of oppression. Extend the sphere, and you take in a greater variety of parties and interests; you make it less probable that a majority of the whole will have a common motive to invade the rights of other citizens.

James Madison, 'Federalist No. 10' [1787], in Richard D. Heffner (ed.), *A Documentary History of the United States* (New York: New American Library, 1952), pp. 38–43.

10. A Republic is Founded on Property

John Adams 1735–1826

Equality and Natural Aristocracy

... what are we to understand ... by equality? Are the citizens to be all of the same age, sex, size, strength, stature, activity, courage, hardiness, industry, patience, ingenuity, wealth, knowledge, fame, wit, temperance, constancy, and wisdom? Was there, or will there ever be, a nation whose individuals were all equal, in natural and acquired qualities, in virtues, talents, and riches? The answer of all mankind must be in the negative. It must then be acknowledged, that in every state, in the Massachusetts, for example, there are inequalities which God and nature have planted there, and which no human legislator ever can eradicate. I should have chosen to have mentioned Virginia, as the most ancient state, or indeed any other in the Union, rather than the one that gave me birth, if I were not afraid of putting suppositions which may give offence, a liberty which my neighbors will pardon. Yet I shall say nothing that is not applicable to all the other twelve.

In this society of Massachusettensians then, there is, it is true, a moral and political equality of rights and duties among all the individuals, and as yet no appearance of artificial inequalities of condition, such as hereditary dignities, titles, magistracies, or legal distinctions; and no established marks, as stars, garters, crosses, or ribbons; there are, nevertheless, inequalities of great moment in the consideration of a legislator, because they have a natural and inevitable influence in society. Let us enumerate some of them: – 1. There is an inequality of *wealth*; some individuals, whether by descent from their ancestors, or from greater skill, industry, and success in business, have estates both in lands and goods of great value; others have no property at all ...

2. *Birth.* Let no man be surprised that this species of inequality is introduced here. Let the page in history be quoted where any nation,

ancient or modern, civilized or savage, is mentioned, among whom no difference was made between the citizens on account of their extraction ...

Definition of Republic

The elements and definitions in most of the arts and sciences are understood alike, by men of education, in all the nations of Europe; but in the science of legislation, which is not one of the least importance to be understood, there is a confusion of languages, as if men were but lately come from Babel. Scarcely any two writers, much less nations, agree in using words in the same sense. Such a latitude, it is true, allows a scope for politicians to speculate, like merchants with false weights, artificial credit, or base money, and to deceive the people, by making the same word adored by one party, and execrated by another. The union of the people, in any principle, rule, or system, is thus rendered impossible; because superstition, prejudice, habit, and passions, are so differently attached to words, that you can scarcely make any nation understand itself ...

... of all the words in all languages, perhaps there has been none so much abused in this way as the words *republic, commonwealth,* and *popular state.* In the *Rerum-Publicarum Collectio,* of which there are fifty and odd volumes, and many of them very incorrect, France, Spain, and Portugal, the four great empires, the Babylonian, Persian, Greek, and Roman, and even the Ottoman, are all denominated republics. If, indeed, a republic signifies nothing but public affairs, it is equally applicable to all nations; and every kind of government, despotisms, monarchies, aristocracies, democracies, and every possible or imaginable composition of them are all republics. There is, no doubt, a public good and evil, a commonwealth and a common impoverishment in all of them. Others define a republic to be a government of more than one. This will exclude only the despotisms; for a monarchy administered by laws, requires at least magistrates to register them, and consequently more than one person in the government. Some comprehend under the term only aristocracies and democracies, and mixtures of these, without any distinct executive power. Others, again, more rationally, define a public to signify only a government, in which all men, rich and poor, magistrates and subjects, officers and people, masters and servants, the first citizen and the last, are equally subject to the laws. This, indeed, appears to be the true and only true definition of a republic. The word *res,* every one knows, signified in the Roman language wealth, riches, property; the word *publicus,* quasi populicus, and per syncope pôplicus, signified public, common, belonging to the people; *res publica,* therefore, was publica res, the wealth, riches, or property of the people. *Res populi,* and the original meaning of the word *republic* could be no other than a government in which the property of the people predominated and governed; and it had more relation to property than liberty. It signified a government, in which the property of the public, or people, and of every one of them, was secured and protected by law. This idea, indeed, implies liberty; because property cannot be secure unless the man be at liberty to acquire, use, or part with it, at his discretion, and unless he have his personal liberty of life and limb, motion and rest, for that purpose. It implies, moreover, that the property and liberty of all men, not merely of a majority, should be safe; for the people, or public, comprehends more than a majority, it comprehends all and every individual; and the property of every citizen is a part of the public property, as each citizen is a part of the public, people, or community. The property, therefore, of every man has a share in government, and is more powerful than any citizen, or party of citizens; it is governed only by the law.

John Adams, 'A Defence of the Constitution of the United States of America' [1787–8], in Adrienne Koch (ed.), *The American Enlightenment* (New York: George Braziller, 1965), pp. 261, 263–5.

11. Friends and Fellow Citizens

George Washington 1732–99

Friends and Fellow-Citizens:
The period for a new election of a citizen to administer the Executive Government of the United States being not far distant, and the time actually arrived when your thoughts must be employed in designating the person who is to be clothed with that important trust, it appears to me proper, especially as it may conduce to a more distinct expression of the public voice, that I should now apprise you of the resolution I have formed to decline being considered among the number of those out of whom a choice is to be made ...

A solicitude for your welfare which can not end with my life, and the apprehension of danger natural to that solicitude, urge me on an occasion like the present to offer to your solemn contemplation and to recommend to your frequent review some sentiments which are the result of much reflection, of no inconsiderable observation, and which appear to me all important to the permanency of your felicity as a people ...

Interwoven as is the love of liberty with every ligament of your hearts, no recommendation of mine is necessary to fortify or confirm the attachment.

The unity of government which constitutes you one people is also now dear to you. It is justly so, for it is a main pillar in the edifice of your real independence, the support of your tranquillity at home, your peace abroad, of your safety, of your prosperity, of that very liberty which you so highly prize. But as it is easy to foresee that from different causes and from different quarters much pains will be taken, many artifices employed, to weaken in your minds the conviction of this truth, as this is the point in your political fortress against which the batteries of internal and external enemies will be most constantly and actively (though often covertly and insidiously) directed, it is of infinite moment that you should properly estimate the immense value of your national union to your collective and individual happiness; that you should cherish a cordial, habitual, and immovable attachment to it; accustoming yourselves to think and speak of it as of the palladium of your political safety and prosperity; watching for its preservation with jealous anxiety; discountenancing whatever may suggest even a suspicion that it can in any event be abandoned, and indignantly frowning upon the first dawning of every attempt to alienate any portion of our country from the rest or to enfeeble the sacred ties which now link together the various parts.

For this you have every inducement of sympathy and interest. Citizens by birth or choice of a common country, that country has a right to concentrate your affections. The name of American, which belongs to you in your national capacity, must always exalt the just pride of patriotism more than any appellation derived from local discriminations. With slight shades of difference, you have the same religion, manners, habits, and political principles. You have in a common cause fought and triumphed together. The independence and liberty you possess are the work of joint councils and joint efforts, of common dangers, sufferings, and successes ...

While, then, every part of our country thus feels an immediate and particular interest in union, all the parts combined can not fail to find in the united mass of means and efforts greater strength, greater resource, proportionably greater security from external danger, a less frequent interruption of their peace by foreign nations, and what is of inestimable value, they must derive from union an exemption from those broils and wars between themselves which so frequently afflict neighboring countries not tied together by the same governments, which their own rivalships alone would be sufficient to produce, but which opposite foreign alliances, attachments, and intrigues would stimulate and imbitter. Hence, likewise, they will avoid the necessity of those overgrown military establishments which, under any form of government, are inauspicious to liberty, and which are to be regarded as particularly hostile to republican liberty. In this sense it is that your union ought to be considered as a main prop of your liberty, and that the love of the one ought to endear to you the preservation of the other ...

Is there a doubt whether a common government can embrace so large a sphere? Let experience solve it. To listen to mere speculation in such a case were criminal. It is well worth a fair and full experiment. With such powerful and obvious motives to union affecting all parts of our country, while experience shall not have demonstrated its impracticability, there will always be reason to distrust the patriotism of those who in any quarter may endeavor to weaken its bands ...

Toward the preservation of your Government and the permanency of your present happy state, it is requisite not only that you steadily discountenance irregular oppositions to its acknowledged authority, but also that you resist with care the spirit of innovation upon its principles, however specious the pretexts. One method of assault may be to effect in the forms of the Constitutions alterations which will impair the energy of the system, and thus to undermine what can not be directly overthrown. In all the changes to which you may be invited remember that time and habit are at least as necessary to fix the true character of governments as of other human institutions; that experience is the surest standard by which to test the real tendency of the existing constitution of a country; that facility in changes upon the credit of mere hypothesis and opinion exposes to perpetual change, from the endless variety of hypothesis and opinion; and remember especially that for the efficient management of your common interests in a country so extensive as ours a government of as much vigor as is consistent with the perfect security of liberty is indispensable. Liberty itself will find in such a government, with powers properly distributed and adjusted, its surest guardian. It is, indeed, little else than a name where the government is too feeble to withstand the enterprises of faction, to confine each member of the society within the limits prescribed by the laws, and to maintain all in the secure and tranquil enjoyment of the rights of person and property.

I have already intimated to you the danger of parties in the State, with particular reference to the founding of them on geographical discriminations. Let me now take a more comprehensive view, and warn you in the most solemn manner against the baneful effects of the spirit of party generally.

This spirit, unfortunately, is inseparable from our nature, having its root in the strongest passions of the human mind. It exists under different shapes in all governments, more or less stifled, controlled, or repressed; but in those of the popular form it is seen in its greatest rankness and is truly their worst enemy ...

It serves always to distract the public councils and enfeeble the public administration. It agitates the community with ill-founded jealousies and false alarms; kindles the animosity of one part against another; foments occasionally riot and insurrection. It opens the door to foreign influence and corruption, which find a facilitated access to the government itself through the channels of party passion. Thus the policy and the will of one country are subjected to the policy and will of another ...

It is substantially true that virtue or morality is a necessary spring of popular government. The rule indeed extends with more or less force to every species of free government. Who that is a sincere friend to it can look with indifference upon attempts to shake the foundation of the fabric? Promote, then, as an object of primary importance, institutions for the general diffusion of knowledge. In proportion as the structure of a government gives force to public opinion, it is essential that public opinion should be enlightened.

George Washington, 'Farewell Address', September 1796.

12. We Are All Republicans

Thomas Jefferson 1743–1826

Friends and Fellow Citizens:

Called upon to undertake the duties of the first executive office of our country, I avail myself of the presence of that portion of my fellow-citizens which is here assembled to express my grateful thanks for the favor with which they have been pleased to look toward me, to declare a sincere consciousness that the task is above my talents, and that I approach it with those anxious and awful presentiments which the greatness of the charge and the weakness of my powers so justly inspire. A rising nation, spread over a wide and fruitful land, traversing all the seas with the rich productions of their industry, engaged in commerce with nations who feel power and forget right, advancing rapidly to destinies beyond the reach of mortal eye – when I contemplate these transcendent objects, and see the honor, the happiness, and the hopes of this beloved country committed to the issue and the auspices of this day, I shrink from the contemplation, and humble myself before the magnitude of the undertaking. Utterly, indeed, should I despair did not the presence of many whom I here see remind me that in the other high authorities provided by our Constitution I shall find resources of wisdom, of virtue, and of zeal on which to rely under all difficulties. To you, then, gentlemen, who are charged with the sovereign functions of legislation, and to those associated with you, I look with encouragement for that guidance and support which may enable us to steer with safety the vessel in which we are all embarked amidst the conflicting elements of a troubled world.

During the contest of opinion through which we have passed the animation of discussions and of exertions has sometimes worn an aspect which might impose on strangers unused to think freely and to speak and to write what they think; but this being now decided by the voice of the nation, announced according to the rules of the Constitution, all will, of course, arrange themselves under the will of the law, and unite in common efforts for the common good. All, too, will bear in mind this sacred principle, that though the will of the majority is in all cases to prevail, that will to be rightful must be reasonable; that the minority possess their equal rights, which equal law must protect, and to violate would be oppression. Let us, then, fellow-citizens, unite with one heart and one mind. Let us restore to social intercourse that harmony and affection without which liberty and even life itself are but dreary things. And let us reflect that, having banished from our land that religious intolerance under which mankind so long bled and suffered, we have yet gained little if we countenance a political intolerance as despotic, as wicked, and capable of as bitter and bloody persecutions. During the throes and convulsions of the ancient world, during the agonizing spasms of infuriated man, seeking through blood and slaughter his long-lost liberty, it was not wonderful that the agitation of the billows should reach even this distant and peaceful shore; that this should be more felt and feared by some and less by others, and should divide opinions as to measures of safety. But every difference of opinion is not a difference of principle. We have called by different names brethren of the same principle. We are all Republicans, we are all Federalists. If there be any among us who would wish to dissolve this Union or to change its republican form, let them stand undisturbed as monuments of the safety with which error of opinion may be tolerated where reason is left free to combat it. I know, indeed, that some honest men fear that a republican government can not be strong, that this Government is not strong enough; but would the honest patriot, in the full tide of successful experiment, abandon a government which has so far kept us free and firm on the theoretic and visionary fear that this Government, the world's best hope, may by possibility want energy to preserve itself? I trust not. I believe this, on the contrary, the strongest Government on earth. I believe it the only one where every man, at the call of the law, would fly to the standard of the law, and would meet invasions of the public order as his own personal concern. Sometimes it is said that man can not be trusted with the government of himself. Can he, then, be trusted with the government of others? Or have we found angels in the forms of kings to govern him? Let history answer this question.

Let us, then, with courage and confidence pursue our own Federal and Republican principles, our attachment to union and representative government. Kindly separated by nature and a wide ocean from the exterminating havoc of one quarter of the globe; too high-minded to endure the degradations of the others; possessing a chosen country, with room enough for our descendants to the thousandth and thousandth generation; entertaining a due sense of our equal right to the use of our own faculties, to the acquisitions of our own industry, to honor and confidence from our fellow-citizens, resulting not from birth, but from our actions and their sense of them; enlightened by a benign religion, professed, indeed, and practiced in various forms, yet all of them inculcating honesty, truth, temperance, gratitude, and the love of man; acknowledging and adoring an overruling Providence, which by all its dispensations proves that it delights in the happiness of man here and his greater happiness hereafter – with all these blessings, what more is necessary to make us a happy and a prosperous people? Still one thing more, fellow-citizens – a wise and frugal Government, which shall restrain men from injuring one another, shall leave them otherwise free to regulate their own pursuits of industry and improvement, and shall not take from the mouth of labor the bread it has earned. This is the sum of good government, and this is necessary to close the circle of our felicities.

About to enter, fellow-citizens, on the exercise of duties which comprehend everything dear and valuable to you, it is proper you should understand what I deem the essential principles of our Government, and consequently those which ought to shape its Administration. I will compress them within the narrowest compass they will bear, stating the general principle, but not all its limitations. Equal and exact justice to all men, of whatever state or persuasion, religious or political; peace, commerce, and honest friendship with all nations, entangling alliances with none; the support of the State governments in all their rights, as the most competent administrations for our domestic concerns and the surest bulwarks against antirepublican tendencies; the preservation of the General Government in its whole constitutional vigor, as the sheet anchor of our peace at home and safety abroad; a jealous care of the right of election by the people – a mild and safe corrective of abuses which are lopped by the sword of revolution where peaceable remedies are unprovided; absolute acquiescence in the decisions of the majority, the vital principle of republics, from which is no appeal but to force, the vital principle and immediate parent of despotism; a well-disciplined militia, our best reliance in peace and for the first moments of war, till regulars may relieve them; the supremacy of the civil over the military authority; economy in the public expense, that labor may be lightly burthened; the honest payment of our debts and sacred preservation of the public faith; encouragement of agriculture, and of commerce as its handmaid; the diffusion of information and arraignment of all abuses at the bar of the public reason; freedom of religion; freedom of the press, and freedom of person under the protection of the habeas corpus, and trial by juries impartially selected. These principles form the bright constellation which has gone before us and guided our steps through an age of revolution and reformation. The wisdom of our sages and blood of our heroes have been devoted to their attainment. They should be the creed of our political faith, the text of civic instruction, the touchstone by which to try the services of those we trust; and should we wander from them in moments of error or of alarm, let us hasten to retrace our steps and to regain the road which alone leads to peace, liberty, and safety.

Thomas Jefferson, 'We are All Republicans, We are All Federalists', first inaugural address, 4 March 1801.

13. Human Emancipation

Karl Marx 1818–83

Where the political State has attained to its true development, the individual leads not only in thought, in consciousness, but in reality, a double life, a heavenly and an earthly life, a life in the political community, wherein he counts as a member of the community, and a life in bourgeois society, wherein he is active as a private person, regarding other men as a means, degrading himself into a means and becoming a plaything of alien powers.

The political State is related to bourgeois society as spiritualistically as heaven is to earth. It occupies the same position of antagonism towards bourgeois society; it subdues the latter just as religion overcomes the limitations of the profane world, that is, by recognising bourgeois society and allowing the latter to dominate it. Man in his outermost reality, in bourgeois society, is a profane being. Here, where he is a real individual for himself and others, he is an untrue phenomenon.

In the State, on the other hand, where the individual is a species-being, he is the imaginary member of an imaginary sovereignty, he is robbed of his real individual life and filled with an unreal universality.

The conflict in which the individual as the professor of a particular religion is involved with his citizenship, with other individuals as members of the community, reduces itself to the secular cleavage between the political State and bourgeois society.

For the individual as a bourgeois 'life in the State is only a semblance, or a passing exception to the rule and the nature of things'. In any case, the bourgeois, like the Jew, remains only sophistically in political life, just as the citizen remains a Jew or a bourgeois only sophistically. It is the sophistry of the political State itself. The difference between the religious individual and the citizen is the difference between the merchant and the citizen, between the labourer and the citizen, between the landowner and the citizen, between the living individual and the citizen. The contradiction in which the religious individual is involved with the political individual, is the same contradiction in which the bourgeois is involved with the citizen, in which the member of bourgeois society is involved with his political lionskin ...

Political emancipation at least represents important progress; while not the last form of human emancipation generally, it is the last form of human emancipation within the existing world order. It is understood that we are speaking here of real, of practical emancipation ...

But there is no misunderstanding about the limits of political emancipation. The division of the individual into a public and a private individual, the expulsion of religion from the State into bourgeois society, is not a step, it is the completion of political emancipation, which thus neither abolishes nor seeks to abolish the real religiosity of the individual.

The splitting-up of the individual into Jew and citizen, into Protestant and citizen, into a religious person and citizen, this decomposition does not belie citizenship; it is not a circumvention of political emancipation; it is political emancipation itself, it is the political manner of becoming emancipated from religion. Moreover, in times when the political State as a political State is forcibly born of bourgeois society, when human self-liberation strives to realise itself under the form of political self-liberation, the State is driven the whole length of abolishing, of destroying religion, but it also proceeds to the abolition of private property, to the law of maximum, to confiscation, to progressive taxation, just as it proceeds to the abolition of life, to the guillotine. In the moment of its heightened consciousness, the political life seeks to suppress its fundamental conditions, bourgeois society and its elements, and to constitute itself as the real and uncontradictory species-life of the individual. It is, however, only able to do this by a flagrant violation of its own conditions of life, by declaring the revolution to be permanent and the political drama therefore ends as inevitably with the restoration of religion, of private property, and all the elements of bourgeois society, as war ends with peace.

... that political emancipation is not human emancipation. If you Jews desire to be politically emancipated, without emancipating yourselves humanly, the incompleteness, the contradiction, lies not only in you, but it also resides in the essence and the category of political emancipation ...

Let us consider for a moment the so-called rights of man, in fact the rights of man in their authentic shape, in the shape which they possess among their discoverers, the North Americans and the French. In part these rights of man are political rights, rights which are only exercised in the community with others. Participation in the affairs of the community, in fact of the political community, forms their substance. They come within the category of political freedom, of civil rights, which does not, as we have seen, presuppose the unequivocal and positive abolition of religion, and therefore of Judaism. It remains to consider the other aspect of human rights, the *droits de l'homme* apart from the *droits du citoyen* ...

The rights of man as such are distinguished from the rights of the citizen. What is this man apart from the citizen? Nothing else than a member of bourgeois society. Why is the member of bourgeois society called 'man', and why are his rights called the rights of man? How do we explain this fact? From the relation of the political State to bourgeois society, and from the meaning of political emancipation.

Above all we must record the fact that the so-called rights of man, as distinguished from the rights of the citizen, are nothing else than the rights of the member of bourgeois society, that is, of the egoistic individual, of man separated from man and the community ...

None of the so-called rights of man, therefore, goes beyond the egoistic individual, beyond the individual as a member of bourgeois society, withdrawn into his private interests and separated from the community. Far from regarding the individual as a species being, the species-life, Society itself, rather appears as an external frame for the individual, as a limitation of his original independence. The sole bond which connects him with his fellows is natural necessity, material needs and private interest, the preservation of his property and his egoistic person ...

The political emancipation is at the same time the dissolution of the old society, upon which was based the civic society, or the rulership alienated from the people. The political revolution is the revolution of bourgeois society. What was the character of the old society? It can be described in one word. Feudality. The old civic society had a directly political character, that is, the elements of civic life, as for example property or the family, or the mode and kind of labour, were raised to the level of elements of the community in the form of landlordism, status, and corporation. In this form they determined the relation of the individual to the community, that is, his political relation, his relationship of separation and exclusion from the other constituent parts of society ...

But the completion of the idealism of the State was at the same time the completion of the materialism of civic society.

The throwing off of the political yoke was at the same time the throwing off of the bond which had curbed the egoistic spirit of civic society. The political emancipation was at the same time an emancipation of civic society from politics, from even the semblance of a general content.

Feudal society was resolved into its basic elements, its individual members. But into the individuals who really formed its basis, that is, the egoistic individual.

This individual, the member of civic society, is now the basis, the assumption of the political State. He is recognised as such in the rights of man.

The liberty of the egoistic individual and the recognition of this liberty are, however, tantamount to the recognition of the unbridled movement of the intellectual and material elements which inform him ...

But the individual as a member of civic society, the unpolitical individual, necessarily appears as the natural individual. The rights of man appear as natural rights, for the self-conscious activity concentrates itself upon the political act. The egoistic individual is the sediment of the dissolved society, the object of immediate certitude, and therefore a natural object ... the individual as a member of bourgeois society counts as the proper individual as man in contradistinction to the citizen, because he is a man in his sensual, individual, closest existence, whereas political man is only the abstract, artificial individual, the individual as an allegorical, moral person. The real man is only recognised in the shape of the egoistic individual, the true man is only recognised in the shape of the abstract citizen ...

All emancipation leads back to the human world, to relationships, to men themselves.

Political emancipation is a reduction of man, on the one side to the member of bourgeois society, to the egoistic, independent individual, and on the other side, to the citizen, to the moral person.

Not until the real, individual man is identical with the citizen, and has become a species-being in his empirical life, in his individual work, in his individual relationships, not until man has recognised and organised his own capacities as social capacities, and consequently the social force is no longer divided by the political power, not until then will human emancipation be achieved.

MEGA 1/2 March 1843–August 1844 (Berlin: Deitz Verlag, 1982), pp. 141–62. The translation here is based on that of H.J. Stenning in *Selected Essays by Karl Marx* (London: Leonard Parsons, 1926), pp. 55–85.

14. Some Are More Equal Than Others

Dred Scott v. Sandford [1857] United States Supreme Court

The question is simply this: can a negro, whose ancestors were imported into this country and sold as slaves, become a member of the political community formed and brought into existence by the Constitution of the United States, and as such become entitled to all the rights, and privileges, and immunities, guarantied by that instrument to the citizen. One of these rights is the privilege of suing in a court of the United

States in the cases specified in the Constitution.

It will be observed, that the plea applies to that class of persons only whose ancestors were negroes of the African race, and imported into this country, and sold and held as slaves. The only matter in issue before the court, therefore, is, whether the descendants of such slaves, when they shall be emancipated, or who are born of parents who had become free before their birth, are citizens of a state, in the sense in which the word 'citizen' is used in the Constitution of the United States ...

The words 'people of the United States' and 'citizens' are synonymous terms, and mean the same thing. They both describe the political body, who, according to our republican institutions, form the sovereignty, and who hold the power and conduct the government through their representatives. They are what we familiarly call the 'sovereign people,' and every citizen is one of this people, and a constituent member of this sovereignty. The question before us is, whether the class of persons described in the plea in abatement compose a portion of this people, and are constituent members of this sovereignty. We think they are not, and that they are not included, and were not intended to be included, under the word 'citizens' in the Constitution, and can, therefore, claim none of the rights and privileges which that instrument provides for and secures to citizens of the United States. On the contrary, they were at that time considered as a subordinate and inferior class of beings, who had been subjugated by the dominant race, and whether emancipated or not, yet remained subject to their authority, and had no rights or privileges but such as those who held the power and the government might choose to grant them ...

In discussing this question, we must not confound the rights of citizenship which a State may confer within its own limits, and the rights of citizenship as a member of the Union. It does not by any means follow, because he has all the rights and privileges of a citizen of a State, that he must be a citizen of the United States. He may have all the rights and privileges of the citizen of a State, and yet not be entitled to the rights and privileges of a citizen in any other State. For, previous to the adoption of the Constitution of the United States, every State had the undoubted right to confer on whomsoever it pleased the character of a citizen, and to endow him with all its rights. But this character, of course, was confined to the boundaries of the State, and gave him no rights or privileges in other States beyond those secured to him by the laws of nations and the comity of States. Nor have the several States surrendered the power of conferring these rights and privileges by adopting the Constitution of the United States. Each State may still confer them upon an alien, or any one it thinks proper, or upon any class or description of persons; yet he would not be a citizen in the sense in which that word is used in the Constitution of the

United States, nor entitled to sue as such in one of its courts, nor to the privileges and immunities of a citizen in the other States. The rights which he would acquire would be restricted to the State which gave them ...

It is very clear, therefore, that no State can, by any Act or law of its own, passed, since the adoption of the Constitution, introduce a new member into the political community created by the Constitution of the United States. It cannot make him a member of this community by making him a member of its own. And for the same reason it cannot introduce any person, or description of persons, who were not intended to be embraced in this new political family, which the Constitution brought into existence, but were intended to be excluded from it.

The question then arises, whether the provisions of the Constitution, in relation to the personal rights and privileges to which the citizen of a state should be entitled, embraced the negro African race, at that time in this country, or who might afterwards be imported, who had then or should afterwards be made free in any State; and to put it in the power of a single State to make him a citizen of the United States, and endue him with the full rights of citizenship in every other State without their consent. Does the Constitution of the United States act upon him whenever he shall be made free under the laws of a State, and raised there to the rank of a citizen, and immediately clothe him with all the privileges of a citizen in every other State, and in its own courts?

The court think the affirmative of these propositions cannot be maintained. And if it cannot, the plaintiff in error could not be a citizen of the State of Missouri, within the meaning of the Constitution of the United States, and, consequently, was not entitled to sue in its courts ...

In the opinion of the court, the legislation and histories of the times, and the language used in the Declaration of Independence, show, that neither the class of persons who had been imported as slaves, nor their descendants, whether they had become free or not, were then acknowledged as a part of the people, nor intended to be included in the general words used in that memorable instrument.

... there are two clauses in the Constitution which point directly and specifically to the negro race as a separate class of persons, and show clearly that they were not regarded as a portion of the people or citizens of the government then formed.

One of these clauses reserves to each of the thirteen States the right to import slaves until the year 1808, if it thinks proper. And the importation which it thus sanctions was unquestionably of persons of the race of which we are speaking, as the traffic in slaves in the United States had always been confined to them. And by the other provision the States pledge themselves to each other to maintain the right of property of the master, by delivering up to him any slave who may have escaped from his service, and be found within their respective territories ...

And these two provisions show, conclusively, that neither the description of persons therein referred to, nor their descendants, were embraced in any of the other provisions of the Constitution; for certainly these two clauses were not intended to confer on them or their posterity the blessings of liberty, or any of the personal rights so carefully provided for the citizen ...

Indeed, when we look to the condition of this race in the several States at the time, it is impossible to believe that these rights and privileges were intended to be extended to them ...

The legislation of the States therefore shows, in a manner not to be mistaken, the inferior and subject condition of that race at the time the Constitution was adopted, and long afterwards, throughout the thirteen States by which that instrument was framed; and it is hardly consistent with the respect due to these States, to suppose that they regarded at that time, as fellow-citizens and members of the sovereignty, a class of beings whom they had thus stigmatized ...

Upon a full and careful consideration of the subject, the court is of opinion that, upon the facts stated in the plea in abatement, Dred Scott was not a citizen of Missouri within the meaning of the Constitution of the United States, and not entitled as such to sue in its courts.

Chief Justice Roger B. Taney for the US Supreme Court, *Dred Scott* v. *Sandford* [1857], in *United States Supreme Court Reports*, 15 Law edn, pp. 700–1, 703, 709–10.

Part VII

Citizen and State

1. To Live Without Duties is Obscene

Ralph Waldo Emerson 1803–82

It will be agreed everywhere that society must have the benefit of the best leaders. How to obtain them? Birth has been tried and failed. Caste in India has no good result. Ennobling of one family is good for one generation; not sure beyond. Slavery had mischief enough to answer for, but it had this good in it – the pricing of men. In the South a slave was bluntly but accurately valued at five hundred to a thousand dollars, if a good field-hand; if a mechanic, as carpenter or smith, twelve hundred or two thousand. In Rome or Greece what sums would not be paid for a superior slave, a confidential secretary and manager, an educated slave; a man of genius, a Moses educated in Egypt? I don't know how much Epictetus was sold for, or Æsop, or Toussaint l'Ouverture, and perhaps it was not a good market-day. Time was, in England, when the state stipulated beforehand what price should be paid for each citizen's life, if he was killed. Now, if it were possible, I should like to see that appraisal applied to every man, and every man made acquainted with the true number and weight of every adult citizen, and that he be placed where he belongs, with so much power confided to him as he could carry and use.

In the absence of such anthropometer I have a perfect confidence in the natural laws. I think that the community – every community, if obstructing laws and usages are removed – will be the best measure and the justest judge of the citizen, or will in the long run give the fairest verdict and reward; better than any royal patronage; better than any premium on race; better than any statute elevating families to hereditary distinction, or any class to sacerdotal education and power. The verdict of battles will best prove the general; the town-meeting, the Congress, will not fail to find out legislative talent. The prerogatives of a right physician are determined, not by his diplomas, but by the health he restores to body and mind; the powers of a geometer by solving his problem; of a priest by the act of inspiring us with a sentiment which disperses the grief from which we suffered. When the lawyer tries his case in court he himself is also on trial and his own merits appear as well as his client's. When old writers are consulted by young writers who have written their first book, they say, Publish it by all means; so only can you certainly know its quality.

But we venture to put any man in any place. It is curious how negligent the public is of the essential qualifications of its representatives. They ask if a man is a Republican, a Democrat? Yes. Is he a man of talent? Yes. Is he honest and not looking for an office or any manner of bribe? He is honest. Well then choose him by acclamation. And they go home and tell their wives with great satisfaction what a good thing they have done. But they forgot to ask the fourth question, not less important than either of the others, and without which the others do not avail. Has he a will? Can he carry his points against opposition. Probably not. It is not sufficient that your work follows your genius, or is organic, to give you the magnetic power over men. More than taste and talent must go to the Will. That must also be a gift of Nature. It is in some; it is not in others. But I should say, if it is not in you, you had better not put yourself in places where not to have it is to be a public enemy.

The expectation and claims of mankind indicate the duties of this class. Some service they must pay. We do not expect them to be saints, and it is very pleasing to see the instinct of mankind on this matter – how much they will forgive to such as pay substantial service and work energetically after their kind; but they do not extend the same indulgence to those who claim and enjoy the same prerogative but render no returns. The day is darkened when the golden river runs down into mud; when genius grows idle and wanton and reckless of its fine duties of being Saint, Prophet, Inspirer to its humble fellows, balks their respect and confounds their understanding by silly extravagances. To a right aristocracy, to Hercules, to Theseus, Odin, the Cid, Napoleon; to Sir Robert Walpole, to Fox, Chatham, Mirabeau, Jefferson, O'Connell – to the men, that is, who are incomparably superior to the populace in ways agreeable to the populace, showing them the way they should go, doing for them what they wish done and cannot do – of course everything will be permitted and pardoned – gaming, drinking, fighting, luxury. These are the heads of party, who can do no wrong – everything short of infamous crime will pass. But if those who merely sit in their places and are not, like them, able; if the dressed and perfumed gentleman, who serves the people in no wise and adorns them not, is not even *not afraid of them*, if such an one go about to set ill examples and corrupt them, who shall blame them if they burn his barns, insult his children, assault his person, and express their unequivocal indignation and contempt? He eats their bread, he does not scorn to live by their labor, and after breakfast he cannot remember that there are human beings. To live without duties is obscene ...

Ralph Waldo Emerson, 'Aristocracy' [1848], in Perry Miller (ed.), *The American Transcendentalists: Their Prose and Poetry* (New York: Doubleday, 1957), pp. 296–300.

2. Time and Duties

Joseph Mazzini 1805–72

Society has greater power, not greater rights, than the individual. How, then, will you prove to the individual that he is bound to confound his will in the will of his brothers, whether of country or of humanity?

By means of the prison or the executioner?

Every society that has existed hitherto has employed these means.

But this is a state of war, and we need peace: this is tyrannical repression, and we need Education.

EDUCATION, I have said, and my whole doctrine is included and summed up in this grand word. The vital question in agitation at the present day is a question of Education. We do not seek to establish a new order of things through violence. Any order of things established through violence, even though in itself superior to the old, is still a tyranny. What we have to do is to propose, for the approval of the nation, an order of things which we believe to be superior to that now existing, and to *educate* men by every possible means to develope it and act in accordance with it.

The theory of Rights may suffice to arouse men to overthrow the obstacles placed in their path by tyranny, but it is impotent where the object in view is to create a noble and powerful harmony between the various elements of which the nation is composed. With the theory of happiness as the primary aim of existence, we shall only produce egotists who will carry the old passions and desires into the new order of things, and introduce corruption into it a few months after. We have therefore to seek a Principle of Education superior to any such theory, and capable of guiding mankind onwards towards their own improvement, of teaching them constancy and self-sacrifice, and of uniting them with their fellow-men, without making them dependent either on the *idea* of a single man or the *force* of the majority.

This principle is DUTY. We must convince men that they are all sons of one sole God, and bound to fulfil and execute one sole law here on earth: that each of them is bound to live, not for himself, but for others; that the aim of existence is, not to be more or less happy, but to make themselves and others more virtuous; that to struggle against injustice and error (wherever they exist), in the name and for the benefit of their brothers, is not only a *right* but a Duty; a duty which may not be neglected without sin, the duty of their whole life.

Working-men, brothers! understand me well. When I say that the consciousness of your rights will never suffice to produce an important and durable progress, I do not ask you to renounce those rights. I merely say that such rights can only exist as a consequence of duties fulfilled, and that we must begin with fulfilling the last in order to achieve the first. And when I say that in proposing happiness, wellbeing, or material interests, as the aim of existence, we run the risk of producing egotists, I do not say that you ought never to occupy yourselves with these; but I do say that the exclusive endeavour after material interests, sought for, not as a *means*, but as an *end*, always leads to disastrous and deplorable results ...

Material ameliorations are essential, and we will strive to obtain them, not because the one thing necessary to man is that he should be well housed and nourished; but because you can neither acquire a true consciousness of your own dignity, nor achieve your own moral development, so long as you are engaged, as at the present day, in a continual struggle with poverty and want.

You labour for ten or twelve hours of the day: how can you find *time* to educate yourselves? The greater number of you scarcely earn enough to maintain yourselves and your families: how can you find *means* to educate yourselves? The frequent interruption and uncertain duration of your work causes you to alternate excessive labour with periods of idleness: how are you to acquire habits of order, regularity, and assiduity? ...

You have no rights of citizenship, nor participation, either of election or vote, in those laws which are to direct your actions and govern your life. How can you feel the sentiment of citizenship, zeal for the welfare of the state, or sincere affection for its laws?

Your poverty frequently involves the impossibility of your obtaining justice like the other classes: how are you to learn to love and respect justice? Society treats you without a shadow of sympathy: how are you to learn sympathy with society?

It is therefore needful that your material condition should be improved, in order that you may morally progress. It is necessary that you should labour less, so that you may consecrate some hours every day to your soul's improvement. It is needful that you should receive such remuneration for your labour as may enable you to accumulate a sufficient saving to tranquillise your minds as to your future; and above all, it is necessary to purify your souls from all reaction, from all sentiment of vengeance, from every thought of injustice, even towards those who have been unjust to you. You are bound, therefore, to strive for all these ameliorations in your condition, and you will obtain them; but you must seek them as a means, not as an end; seek them from a sense of duty, and not merely as a right; seek them in order that you may become more virtuous, not in order that you may be materially happy ...

There are those who seek to put a limit to the rights of the citizen by telling you that the true association is the state, the nation: that you ought all to be members of that association, but that every partial association amongst yourselves is either adverse to the state, or superfluous.

But the state, the nation, only represents the association of the citizens in those matters and in those tendencies which are common to *all* the men who compose it. There are tendencies and aims which do not embrace *all* the citizens, but only a certain number of them. And precisely as the tendencies and the aims which are common to all, constitute the nation; so the tendencies and aims which are common to a portion of the citizens, should constitute special associations.

Moreover – and this is the fundamental basis of the right of association – association is a guarantee for progress. The state represents a certain sum or mass of *principles*, in which the universality of the citizens are agreed at the time of its foundation. Suppose that a new and true principle, a new and rational development of the truths that have given vitality to the state, should be discovered by a few among its citizens. How shall they diffuse the knowledge of this principle, except by association? Suppose that in consequence of scientific discovery, or of new means of communication opened up between peoples and peoples, or from any other cause, a new *interest* should arise among a certain number of the individuals composing the state, how shall they who first perceive this, make their way among the various interests of long standing, unless by uniting their efforts and their means? ...

Association must be peaceful. It may not use other weapons than the apostolate of the spoken and written word. Its object must be to persuade, not to compel. Association must be public. Secret associations – which are a legitimate weapon of defence where there exists neither liberty nor nation – are illegal, and ought to be dissolved, wherever liberty and the inviolability of thought are rights recognised and protected by the country.

As the scope and intent of association is to open the paths of progress, it must be submitted to the examination and judgment of all.

And, finally, association is bound to respect in others those rights which spring from the essential characteristics of human nature. An association which, like the corporations of the middle ages, should violate the rights of labour, or which should tend directly to restrict liberty of conscience, ought to be repressed by the government of the nation.

With these exceptions, liberty of association among the citizens is as sacred and inviolable as that progress of which it is the life.

Every government which attempts to restrain them betrays its social mission, and it becomes the duty of the people first to admonish it, and – all peaceful means being exhausted – to overthrow it.

Such, my brothers, are the bases upon which your duties are founded, the sources from which spring your rights. An infinite number of questions will arise in the course of your civil life, which it is no part of the present work either to foresee, or to assist you in resolving. My sole aim in this book has been to present to you, even as torches to light you on your way, those *Principles* which should guide you through them all, and in the earnest application of which, you will find a method of resolving them for yourselves.

And this I believe I have done.

I have led you to God, as the source of duty and pledge of the equality of man: to the moral law, as the source of all civil laws and basis of your every judgment as to the conduct of those who frame those laws. I have pointed out to you the people – yourselves, ourselves, the universality of the citizens composing the nation – as the sole interpreter of the law, and the source of all political power. I have told you that the fundamental characteristic of the law is progress; progress indefinite and continuous from epoch to epoch; progress in every branch of human activity, in every manifestation of thought, from religion down to industry and to the distribution of wealth. I have described to you your *duties* towards Humanity, your country, your family, and yourselves. And I have deduced those duties from those essential characteristics which constitute the *human* creature, and which it is your task to develope.

These characteristics – inviolable in every man – are: liberty, susceptibility of education, the social tendency, and the capacity for and necessity of progress. And from these characteristics – without which there is neither true *man* nor true *citizen* possible – I have deduced, not your duties, but your rights; and the general character of the government you should seek for your country.

Joseph Mazzini, 'On the Duties of Man' [1860], in *Joseph Mazzini: A Memoir of E.A.V.* (London: Henry S. King, 1875), pp. 270–6, 354–7.

3. A Government of People

Abraham Lincoln 1809–65

Four score and seven years ago our fathers brought forth on this continent, a new nation, conceived in Liberty, and dedicated to the proposition that all men are created equal.

Now we are engaged in a great civil war, testing whether that nation or any nation so conceived and so dedicated, can long endure. We are met on a great battle-field of that war. We have come to dedicate a portion of that field, as a final resting place for those who here gave their lives that that nation might live. It is altogether fitting and proper that we should do this.

But, in a larger sense, we can not dedicate – we can not consecrate – we can not hallow – this ground. The brave men, living and dead, who struggled here, have consecrated it, far above our poor power to add or detract. The world will little note, nor long remember what we say here, but it can never forget what they did here. It is for us the living, rather, to be dedicated here to the unfinished work which they who fought here have thus far so nobly advanced. It is rather for us to be here dedicated to the great task remaining before us – that from these honored dead we take increased devotion to that cause for which they gave the last full measure of devotion – that we here highly resolve that these dead shall not have died in vain – that this nation, under God, shall have a new birth of freedom – and that government of the people, by the people, for the people, shall not perish from the earth.

Abraham Lincoln, 'The Gettysburg Address', 19 November 1863.

4. A Good American Citizen

Theodore Roosevelt 1858–1919

Of course, in one sense, the first essential for a man's being a good citizen is his possession of the home virtues of which we think when we call a man by the emphatic adjective of manly. No man can be a good citizen who is not a good husband and a good father, who is not honest in his dealings with other men and women, faithful to his friends and fearless in the presence of his foes, who has not got a sound heart, a sound mind, and a sound body; exactly as no amount of attention to civic duties will save a nation if the domestic life is undermined, or there is lack of the rude military virtues which alone can assure a country's position in the world. In a free republic the ideal citizen must be one willing and able to take arms for the defense of the flag, exactly as the ideal citizen must be the father of many healthy children. A race must be strong and vigorous; it must be a race of good fighters and good breeders, else its wisdom will come to naught and its virtue be ineffective; and no sweetness and delicacy, no love for and appreciation of beauty in art or literature, no capacity for building up material prosperity, can possibly atone for the lack of the great virile virtues.

But this is aside from my subject, for what I wish to talk of is the attitude of the American citizen in civic life. It ought to be axiomatic in this country that every man must devote a reasonable share of his time to doing his duty in the political life of the community. No man has a right to shirk his political duties under whatever plea of pleasure or business; and while such shirking may be pardoned in those of small means, it is entirely unpardonable in those among whom it is most common – in the people whose circumstances give them freedom in the struggle for life. In so far as the community grows to think rightly, it will likewise grow to regard the young man of means who shirks his duty to the State in time of peace as being only one degree worse than the man who thus shirks it in time of war. A great many of our men in business, or of our young men who are bent on enjoying life (as they have a perfect right to do if only they do not sacrifice other things to enjoyment), rather plume themselves upon being good citizens if they even vote; yet voting is the very least of their duties. Nothing worth gaining is ever gained without effort. You can no more have freedom without striving and suffering for it than you can win success as a banker or a lawyer without labor and effort, without self-denial in youth and the display of a ready and alert intelligence in middle age. The people who say that they have not time to attend to politics are simply saying that they are unfit to live in a free community. Their place is under a despotism; or if they are content to do nothing but vote, you can take despotism tempered by an occasional plebescite, like that of the second Napoleon...

The first duty of an American citizen, then, is that he shall work in politics; his second duty is that he shall do that work in a practical manner; and his third is that it shall be done in accord with the highest principles of honor and justice. Of course, it is not possible to define rigidly just the way in which the work shall be made practical. Each man's individual temper and convictions must be taken into account...

I think that we ought to be broad-minded enough to recognize the fact that a good citizen, striving with fearlessness, honesty, and common sense to do his best for the nation, can render service to it in many different ways, and by connection with many different organizations. It is well for a man if he is able conscientiously to feel that his views on the great questions of the day, on such questions as the tariff, finance, immigration, the regulation of the liquor traffic, and others like them, are such as to put him in accord with the bulk of those of his fellow citizens who compose one of the greatest parties: but it is perfectly supposable that he may feel so strongly for or against certain principles held by one party, or certain principles held by the other, that he is unable to give his full adherence to either. In such a case I feel that he has no right to plead this lack of agreement with either party as an excuse for refraining from active political work prior to election. It will, of course, bar him from the primaries of the two leading parties, and preclude him from doing his share in organizing their management; but, unless he is very unfortunate, he can surely find a number of men who are in the same position as himself and who agree with him on some specific piece of political work, and they can turn in practically and effectively long before election to try to do this new piece of work in a practical manner...

In the same way, if a man feels that the politics of his city, for instance, are very corrupt and wants to reform them, it would be an excellent idea for him to begin with his district. If he joins with other people, who thinks as he does, to form a club where abstract political virtue will be discussed he may do a great deal of good ...

But in advising you to be practical and to work hard, must not for one moment be understood as advising you to abandon one iota of your self-respect and devotion to principle. It is a bad sign for the country to see one class of our citizens sneer at practical politicians, and another at Sunday-school politics. No man can do both effective and decent work in public life unless he is a practical politician on the one hand, and a sturdy believer in Sunday-school politics on the other. He must always strive manfully for the best, and yet, like Abraham Lincoln, must often resign himself to accept the best possible.

... in being virtuous he must not become ineffective, and ... he must not excuse himself for shirking his duties by any false plea that he cannot do his duties and retain his self-respect. This is nonsense, he can; and when he urges such a plea it is a mark of mere laziness and self-indulgence. And again, he should beware how he becomes a critic of the actions of others, rather than a doer of deeds himself; and in so far as he does act as a critic (and of course the critic has a great and necessary function) he must beware of indiscriminate censure even more than of indiscriminate praise ...

It may be taken for granted that the man who is always sneering at our public life and our public men is a thoroughly bad citizen, and that what little influence he wields in the community is wielded for evil. The public speaker or the editorial writer, who teaches men of education that their proper attitude toward American politics should be one of dislike or indifference, is doing all he can to perpetuate and aggravate the very evils of which he is ostensibly complaining. Exactly as it is generally the case that when a man bewails the decadence of our civilization he is himself physically, mentally, and morally a first-class type of the decadent, so it is usually the case that when a man is perpetually sneering at American politicians, whether worthy or unworthy, he himself is a poor citizen and a friend of the very forces of evil against which he professes to contend ...

Moreover, the very need of denouncing evil makes it all the more wicked to weaken the effect of such denunciations by denouncing also the good. It is the duty of all citizens, irrespective of party, to denounce, and, so far as may be, to punish crimes against the public on the part of politicians or officials. But exactly as the public man who commits a crime against the public is one of the worst of criminals, so, close on his heels in the race for iniquitous distinction, comes the man who falsely charges the public servant with outrageous wrong-doing; whether it is done with foul-mouthed and foolish directness in the vulgar and violent party organ, or with sarcasm, innuendo, and the half-truths that are worse than lies, in some professed organ of independence. Not only should criticism be honest, but it should be intelligent, in order to be effective ...

Finally, the man who wishes to do his duty as a citizen in our country must be imbued through and through with the spirit of Americanism. I am not saying this as a matter of spread-eagle rhetoric: I am saying it quite soberly as a piece of matter-of-fact, common-sense advice, derived from my own experience of others. Of course, the question of Americanism has several sides. If a man is an educated man, he must show his Americanism by not getting misled into following out and trying to apply all the theories of the political thinkers of other countries, such as Germany and France, to our own entirely different conditions. He must not get a fad, for instance, about responsible government; and above all things he must not, merely because he is intelligent, or a college professor well read in political literature, try to discuss our institutions when he has had no practical knowledge of how they are worked. Again, if he is a wealthy man, a man of means and standing, he must really feel, not merely affect to feel, that no social differences obtain save such as a man can in some way himself make by his own actions ...

Again, questions of race origin, like questions of creed, must not be considered: we wish to do good work, and we are all Americans, pure and simple ...

A man has got to be an American and nothing else; and he has no business to be mixing us up with questions of foreign politics, British or Irish, German or French, and no business to try to perpetuate their language and customs in the land of complete religious toleration and equality. If, however, he does become honestly and in good faith an American, then he is entitled to stand precisely as all other Americans stand, and it is the height of unAmericanism to discriminate against him in any way because of creed or birthplace ...

In facing the future and in striving, each according to the measure of his individual capacity, to work out the salvation of our land, we should be neither timid pessimists nor foolish optimists. We should recognize the dangers that exist and that threaten us: we should neither overestimate them nor shrink from them, but steadily fronting them should set to work to overcome and beat them down. Grave perils are yet to be encountered in the stormy course of the Republic – perils from political corruption, perils from individual laziness, indolence and timidity, perils springing from the greed of the unscrupulous rich, and from the anarchic violence of the thriftless and turbulent poor. There is every reason why we should recognize them, but there is no reason why we should fear them or doubt our capacity to overcome them, if only each will, according to the measure of his ability, do his fully duty, and endeavor so to live as to deserve the high praise of being called a good American citizen.

Theodore Roosevelt, 'The Duties of American Citizenship', address before the Liberal Club, Buffalo, NY, 26 January 1893, in *The Works of Theodore Roosevelt*, vol. XV, memorial edn (New York: Charles Scribner's Sons, 1925), pp. 69–80.

5. The Purpose of the State is to Serve the Citizens

Thomas Hill Green 1836–82

The state then presupposes rights, and rights of individuals. It is a form which society takes in order to maintain them. But rights have no being except in a society of men recognising each other as ἴσοι καὶ ὅμοιοι. They are constituted by that mutual recognition.

The slave thus derives from his social relations a real right which the law of the state refuses to admit. The law cannot prevent him from acting and being treated, within certain limits, as a member of a society of persons freely seeking a common good. Now that capability of living in a certain limited community with a certain limited number of human beings, which the slave cannot be prevented from exhibiting, is in principle a capability of living in community with any other human beings, supposing the necessary training to be allowed; and as every such capability constitutes a right, we are entitled to say that the slave has a right to citizenship, to a recognised equality of freedom with any and every one with whom he has to do, and that in refusing him not only citizenship but the means of training his capability of citizenship, the state is violating a right founded on that common human conscious-ness which is evinced both by the language which the slave speaks, and by actual social relations subsisting between him and others. And on the same principle upon which a state is violating natural rights in maintain-ing slavery, it does the same in using force, except under the necessity of self-defence, against members of another community. Membership of any community is so far, in principle, membership of all communities as to constitute a right to be treated as a freeman by all other men, to be exempt from subjection to force except for prevention of force ...

We have already seen that a right against society, as such, is an impossibility; that every right is derived from some social relation; that a right against any group of associated men depends on association, as ἴσοι καὶ ὅμοιος, with them and with some other men ...

Thus the citizen's rights, e.g. as a husband or head of a family or a holder of property, though such rights, arising out of other social relations than that of citizen to citizen, existed when as yet there was no state, are yet to the citizen derived from the state, from that more highly developed form of society in which the association of the family and that of possessors who respect each other's possessions are included as in a fuller whole; which secures to the citizen his family rights and his rights as a holder of property, but under conditions and limitations which the membership of the fuller whole – the reconciliation of rights arising out of one sort of social capability with those arising out of another – renders necessary. Nor can the citizen have any right against the state, in the sense of a right to act otherwise than as a member of some society, the state being for its members the society of societies, the society in which all their claims upon each other are mutually adjusted.

But what exactly is meant by the citizen's acting 'as a member of his state'? What does the assertion that he can have no right to act otherwise than as a member of his state amount to? Does it mean that he has no right to disobey the law of the state to which he belongs, whatever that law may be? that he is not entitled to exercise his powers in any way that the law forbids and to refuse to exercise them in any way that it commands? This question was virtually dealt with before [sections 100, 101] in considering the justifiability of resistance to an ostensible sovereign. The only unqualified answer that can be given to it is one that may seem too general to be of much practical use, viz. that so far as the laws anywhere or at any time in force fulfil the idea of a state, that can be no right to disobey them; or, that there can be no right to disobey the law of the state except in the interest of the state; i.e. for the purpose of making the state in respect of its actual laws more completely correspond to what it is in tendency or idea, viz. the reconciler and sustainer of the rights that arise out of the social relations of men ...

'Is then,' it may be asked, 'the general judgment as to the requirements of social well-being so absolutely authoritative that no individual right can exist against it? What if according to this judgment the institution of slavery is so necessary that citizens are prohibited by law from teaching slaves to read and from harbouring runaways? or if according to it the maintenance of a certain form of worship is so necessary that no other worship can be allowed and no opinion expressed antagonistic to it? Has the individual no rights against enactments founded on such accepted views of social well-being?' We may answer: A right against society as such, a right to act without reference to the needs or good of society, is an impossibility, since every right depends on some social relation, and a right against any group of associated men depends upon association on some footing of equality with them or with some other men. We saw how the right of the slave really rested on this basis, on a social capacity shown in the footing on which he actually lives with other men. On this principle it would follow, if we regard the state as the sustainer and harmoniser of social relations, that the individual can have no right against the state; that its law must be to him of absolute authority. But in fact, as actual states at best fulfil but partially their ideal function, we cannot apply this rule to practice. The general principle that the citizen must never act otherwise than as a citizen, does not carry with it an obligation under all conditions to conform to the law of his state, since those laws may be inconsistent with the true end of the state as the sustainer and harmoniser of social relations ...

Thus to the question, Has the individual no rights against enactments founded on imperfect views of social well-being? we may answer, He has no rights against them founded on any right to do as he likes. Whatever counter-rights he has must be founded on a relation to the social well-being, and that a relation of which his fellow-citizens are aware. He must be able to point to some public interest, generally recognised as such, which is involved in the exercise of the power claimed by him as a right; to show that it is not the general well-being, even as conceived by his fellow-citizens, but some special interest of a class that is concerned in preventing the exercise of the power claimed. In regard to the right of teaching or harbouring the slave, he must appeal to the actual capacity of the slave for community with other men as evinced in the manner described above, to the recognition of this capacity as shown by the actual behaviour of the citizens in many respects towards the slave, to the addition to social well-being that results from the realisation of this capacity in all who possess it through rights being legally guaranteed to them. In this way he must show that the reference to social well-being, on which is founded the recognition of powers as rights, if fairly and thoroughly carried out, leads to the exercise of powers in favour of the slave, in the manner described, not to the prohibition of that exercise as the supposed law prohibits it. The response which in doing so he elicits from the conscience of fellow-citizens shows that in talking of the slave as 'a man and a brother,' he is exercising what is implicitly his right, though it is a right which has not become explicit through legal enactments. This response supplies the factor of social recognition which, as we have seen, is necessary in order to render the exercise of any power a right.

Thomas Hill Green, 'Lectures on the Principles of Political Obligation: Has the Citizen Rights against the State?' [1882], in *Works of Thomas Green Hill*, ed. R.L. Nettleship, vol. II: *Philosophical Works* (London: Longmans, Green and Co, 1990), pp. 460–5.

6. First and Second Class Citizens

Henry Sidgwick 1838–1900

The 'principle of democracy' ought, I conceive, to relate primarily to the structure of government and not to the mode in which its functions should be exercised.

Limiting ourselves then for the present to the consideration of the structure of government, let us ask how, in this department, we are to define the fundamental principle of democracy. There are, I think, two competing definitions; or perhaps I should rather say two distinct principles, explicitly or implicitly assumed in arguing in favour of political institutions commonly recognised as democratic. One of these, – which I myself accept as a principle that the modern State should aim at realising – is 'that government should rest on the active consent of the citizens'; the other is 'that any one self-supporting and law-abiding citizen is, on the average, as well qualified as another for the work of government.' This latter proposition I in the main reject; but I admit that, according to one view of the proof of the first proposition, the second is to some extent implied, and that where democracy – as defined by the first proposition – is fully developed, there is likely to be a tendency to accept and act upon the second to some extent.

In order to examine the relation between the two propositions, it will be well to define the former more precisely. In the first place, I mean by 'active consent' something quite different from the passive acquiescence, the absence of any conscious desire to change the structure or modify the action of government, which may exist under a pure monarchy or oligarchy no less than under a democracy, wherever the members of the community have lost or have not yet acquired the habit of regarding their government as a condition of life which it is in their power to change. Even in such a society the views and sentiments of the governed ordinarily impose certain limits on their government – there are certain things which the latter abstains from doing for fear of exciting discontent and possible disaster: – but this effect is normally produced without consciousness. By 'active consent,' on the other hand, I imply that the citizens are conscious that they can legitimately alter the structure or the action of their government if a sufficient number of them choose to go through a certain process; so that if they make no effort to alter either, they exercise a distinct act of choice: – they may not like their government or its ways, but they at least prefer not to take the trouble of trying to change them ...

... when we say that a democratic government must be supported by the consent of at least a majority of the citizens, we do not ordinarily mean that this consent should be necessary to the validity of every governmental decision ...

... the democratic principle must practically be limited by confining the authoritative decisions of the people at large to certain matters and certain periodically recurring times; and committing the great majority of governmental decisions to bodies or individuals who must have the power – and, I may add, the duty – of deciding without the active consent of the majority and even against its wish.

The question then arises on what principle, in a democracy, the particular persons should be selected to whom this large part of the work of government which cannot advantageously be undertaken by the people at large is to be entrusted.

Here we have to consider the second definition that I gave of the fundamental principle of democracy, 'that one honest and self-supporting citizen is as well qualified as another for the work of government.' This principle was largely carried out in Athens, and elsewhere in the city-states of ancient Greece, by the method of choosing officials by lot, from among the citizens of unblemished civic character. And though no similar attempt to realise this principle is discernible in modern arrangements for democratic government, it seems necessary to consider it; since it may be plausibly argued that its rejection logically involves the rejection of the principle that government must rest on popular consent. For, it may be urged, if we require special qualifications for the minor decisions which even democracy leaves to particular persons and bodies, we ought to require them still more for the more important decisions reserved to the people at large.

In considering this argument we have to take into account partly intellectual, partly moral qualifications. As regards the intellectual qualifications, the analogy of economic relations may be adduced; since in these it is generally admitted that the judgment of the consumer must be combined with that of the producer to obtain the right result; and in political matters the people as a whole seems to be related to the experts who perform the detailed work of governing, much as the consumers are to the producers in other arts ...

As regards moral qualifications, it would be going too far to say that the 'people' – as politically defined – has no 'sinister interests' opposed to the interests of the community as a whole. It is obvious that in the most democratic state there is a mass of non-voters whose interests may be unduly postponed to those of the voters, that the interests of posterity may be unduly sacrificed to those of the present generation, and that a minority of the voters may be unduly sacrificed to the majority. Still, though the electorate as a body may possibly be swayed by narrow and sectional interests, any particular section of it is, *primâ facie*, more likely to be so swayed; and it may be truly said that the people at large is free from certain sinister interests by which governing persons are liable to be influenced: as the latter are under temptations to confer on themselves emoluments, privileges, and powers beyond what is expedient for the public good, and to extend the work of government in order to increase the mass of these advantages. Hence, there is a strong reason for giving weight to the judgment of the people at large in the decision of these and similar matters, however completely we admit the need of experts for the decision of most details of governmental work.

Henry Sidgwick, ch. XXX, in *Elements of Politics* (London: Macmillan, 1891), pp. 583–9.

7. Becoming a Citizen

John MacCun 1846–1929

It has become something of a commonplace to say that 'the democracy' is insatiable. But, in a very real sense, the wonder is that it is so easily satisfied. Eager enough to get its rights, whether civil or political, it would seem as if it has no sooner won them, than, in strange disregard of possibilities, it settles down as though it had made an end, when in truth it has only made a beginning. For though to be a citizen is to possess rights – in any case, civil rights, and, in a democratic country, political rights as well – to possess rights is not to be a citizen. It is to be merely on the way to become one. Never can it enough be realised, in democracies especially, that men become citizens in truth and in substance, only when they use their rights. We do not make a man the owner of a plot of land by presenting him with so many yards of wire fencing, however carefully barbed; nor do we make him a sportsman by the gift of the best of breech-loaders. No more do we make him a citizen by conferring upon him rights. Rights are not rewards, nor decorations, nor ends in themselves. They are advantages, they are opportunities, they are instruments. And when any man has won them, this means simply, that henceforward he is set on a vantage ground, from which, secure from aggression and unrepressed by tyranny, he may begin to do his duty.

Yet it is just this that seems so often to be forgotten. Men are so enamoured of their rights that they forget that the real value of every right must rise or fall with the use to which the right is put. If the average citizen is quick to remind us that in a free country he is free to say what he pleases, he is not so quick to assure his neighbours, or even himself, of the value of what it pleases him to say. Yet, however priceless this right of free speech may be, when it is the condition of words of independence, wisdom, or consolation, who can doubt that it assumes at most a questionable garb, when degraded into the occasion for unlocking the lips of the babbler and the bore? ...

What thus is true of civil rights may be said, and in some respects more emphatically, of the rights we call political. That a citizen is enabled to vote, or even that he actually records his vote, this is but a beggarly result of the extension of the franchise. The very pith and substance of political citizenship would be gone, were its reality to be measured by the occasions, few and far between, upon which the vote is solicited or recorded. The suggestion is on a par with the doctrine of Rousseau, that Englishmen are truly free only when they are engaged in electing members of Parliament. 'The English are only free during the election of members of Parliament; the members once chosen, the people are slaves, nay, as people they have ceased to exist.' – [Morley's *Rousseau*, p. 334]. It is equally false, equally absurd. Men do not live the real life of political freedom in polling booths. Rousseau's paradox is the opposite of the truth. For the stuff and substance of freedom we must look to the weeks, months, years, that lie in the intervals when we are *not* electing members of Parliament; to the use of these intervals that makes a vote given, the outward sign of political conviction, character and work, or to the abuse of these intervals which levels it down to the meaningless, or mischievous, scratching of a ballot paper. The name and the legal status of citizenship are but an empty inheritance, if they be not the preliminaries to a life which is 'free,' not only in the sense that it is encompassed by the Law's protection, but because, within the charmed circle of rights, it achieves that actual well-being in which lies the real deliverance from bondage. For it is fulness of life and not merely immunity from aggression, which is the test of real freedom. The real freeman is the developed man. Nor can all the rights in the world do more than tell us what we *may* do. Strenuous civic life alone can translate possibility into fact ...

Doubters about democratic franchises are apt to insist that no man should have a vote till he is fit to use it. The necessary rejoinder, however, is, that men can only become fit to have votes by first using them. There is no other way. Preparation there may be, in home, in school, in industrial organisation, in the conduct of business. But these will not suffice. Not so easily is the citizen made. It is as Aristotle has it; the harper is not made otherwise than by harping, nor the just man otherwise than by the doing of just deeds. [*Nicomachean Ethics*, Bk. II. i. 6]. How can it be otherwise here, how can the capable voter be made except by voting capably? Citizenship is, after all, but a larger art; and to teach men to do their duties to the State, the only finally effective plan is to give them duties to the State to do.

It is for this reason that many a believer in Democracy is ready, with an equanimity wrongly construed by his critics as levity or simplicity, to sit unmoved under the warning that a raw Democracy may mismanage; or that even an experienced Democracy may not be the best machine for governing. No one need neglect the warning. But there are, at worst, compensations. And they lie in two considerations. The one is that the end of national existence is not solely, nor even mainly to exhibit to the world the spectacle of the most perfect machine of government; but to develop human beings. And the other is that for this purpose there is no school to equal the arena of active public life – none, at any rate, so varied in its interests, so impersonal in its ends, so stimulating in its issues, so powerful in its attractions. Better surely that men should learn the lesson of political citizenship, even at some cost of blundering, than that they never should learn it at all.

John MacCun, *Ethics of Citizenship* (Glasgow: James Maclehose and Sons, 1894), pp. 70–2, 81–2.

8. The State is Nothing but its Citizens

Sir Henry Jones 1852–1923

Surely the State can be nothing apart from its citizens, except an empty name; and when we speak of its rights over its citizens, or of their duties to it we speak elliptically, meaning their rights over and duties to *one another*, in virtue of their common membership. It is the medium of their rights and duties: a human institution, it is true. For the relations that constitute it are the relations of will to will, or of man to man; but it is nothing more than an institution and a mere product of men's activities. 'We look upon the State,' says Mr. A.C. Bradley, 'as a contrivance for securing (to the individual citizen) the enjoyment of his liberty and the opportunity of pursuing his ends, a contrivance which involves some limitation of his rights, and ought to involve as little as possible. Even when reflection has shown us that there is something theoretically wrong with these ideas, we remain convinced that a happiness or a morality which is imposed upon us from without loses half its value, and that there are spheres of our life and parts of our inward experience into which no one ought to intrude. And if we feel strongly our unity with others, and are willing to admit that social and political institutions have a positive object and not the merely negative one of protection, we emphasize the fact that the character or happiness they are to promote are those of individuals.' (*Hellenica*, p. 189.)

It is not to be denied, on the other hand, that not only the language we employ when we speak of the State but our practical attitude towards it, which is a much more significant and serious matter, is quite inconsistent with the view that the State is 'a contrivance,' or mere instrument and means of purposes which it cannot itself formulate. We speak of its *rights* over its citizens and we discuss their limits; but no one denies them. We speak of its *duties* to its citizens, and we condemn or approve it according as we consider that it neglects or fulfils them. We bring its actions under moral criteria, and we call it just or unjust as it succeeds or fails to correspond to them. We consider that it is capable of moral growth or decay, and that its moral qualities, even more than its external circumstances, determine its destiny for good or ill. Is all this nothing but the language of metaphor? Is it for a metaphor that our soldiers are dying on the battle-fields, and their mourning parents are spending the elixir of their lives? Surely, unless we confine the meaning of the State, as is often done for technical purposes, so as to make it signify nothing more than the Government, representing it as something distinct from the social whole in which we live and move and have our being and which we call 'our country,' we must admit that, in regard to it, in the degree in which we are good citizens, we experience the same moral relations as those which bind us to one another.

That the State is a means for the defence and security of individual rights; that it does nothing and can be nothing *apart* from its individual citizens; that it is beyond all comparison the most significant and potent instrument of their well-being, it is not possible to deny. But does it follow that this truth is the whole truth? If it is an organ and a secular organ for the use of individuals, are not its legislators, judges, soldiers, nay every common citizen at his station and amidst his duties, *its* organs? Whose will do the legislators declare when they convert a parliamentary Bill into an Act? Hardly their own, and hardly that of a mere aggregate of individuals. It is 'our country' as a whole, as a more or less harmonious unit and individuality which says 'I *will*' when Parliament, as its organ, enacts that no child within the four seas shall be starved or neglected or be left untaught. The judge, in like manner, applies his country's laws, and by no means his own; and it is in its service that the dreadful deeds of the soldier may acquire the nobility that comes from the service of a sacred cause.

If we take a complete survey of both sides of the situation, and give due weight to what at least seems to be the fact, that the State is a 'contrivance,' an 'organ,' or a means of its citizens, and also that its citizens are its organs and means, a new question arises. Can both views be true? Is a State a good State, and a citizen a good citizen precisely in the degree to which they are for one another *both* means and ends? Kant regards man as 'a member of the kingdom of ends,' and therefore both 'sovereign and subject,' and most truly sovereign when his service is most devoted and self-forgetful – 'counting all things but loss for the excellency' of the moral good. The solution of the problem of the nature of the State lies, I believe, in this direction; that is to say, in the clearer recognition that it is a moral agent, and that its service, in consequence, is the way of the better life for its citizens ...

Surely, it is argued, there is a wider and more generous and more noble service than that of the State, namely, that of humanity; and a good man is something more and better than a good citizen. There are circumstances in which his duty may be to resist the claims of his own country and refuse obedience to its laws, and even to endeavour to overturn it.

The qualification, then, that our sovereign State is moral does not seem to improve matters, for its sovereignty is still absolute; and the service of such a State seems still to enslave, for its citizens are still means.

What answer shall we make? We shall find a clue to it by distinguishing between two meanings of 'liberty' which are often confused: one of them the lowest, and an object of disapproval whether in men or States, namely, the liberty that recognizes no law and is best called 'licence'; and the other the highest, which recognizes and adopts a law that is absolute and universal, and by its adoption of it converts it into the law of its own life, and its rigour into 'a delight.' 'I will walk at liberty' or 'at large,' 'for I seek thy precepts.' 'Thy statutes have been my songs in the house of my pilgrimage' [Ps. cxix. 45, 54]. This latter is a liberty that breaks into dithyrambs, it is so full and free and joyous. And it is this liberty which the good citizen desires for himself and respects in others, and for the sake of which States, rising at last to the dignity of their own nature as moral, have armed themselves with the weapons of destruction and staked their existence ...

There is a similar ambiguity in the conception of 'Personality' or individuality, which is attributed to the State by all who claim for it any kind of sovereignty, or speak of its 'rights,' whether over its citizens or against other States. We have said that 'personality' is an object of respect, whether we speak of the personality of an individual or of a State. But that respect or reverence may be based on two opposite views of 'Personality' or the self; namely, either on its privacy and exclusiveness, or upon its comprehensiveness. For the self or a 'person' has both of these characters. 'Each self,' we are told, 'is a unique existence, which is perfectly *impervious* to other selves – impervious in a fashion of which the impenetrability of matter is a faint analogue. The self, accordingly, resists invasion; in its character of self it refuses to admit another self within itself, and thus be made, as it were, a mere retainer of something else ... The very principle of a self is this exclusiveness ...

The study of the Greek State is the beginning of political wisdom, and every enquirer must draw water from this limpid little well in the hinterland of the political past of the race. But the stream has broadened and now fertilizes a wider country; and it carries with it a spiritual commerce beyond the dream of Greece. It will serve our purpose to ask what grounds can be discovered in our own State on which it may rest its title to reverence from its citizens. And the shortest way of answering is possibly to ask not what the State has done for its citizens, but what it has *not* done. 'What have you,' I may ask, 'which is not the gift of your country?'

'I have my individuality,' you reply, 'and its indefeasible rights, which the State must in all circumstances respect.' And the answer is sound: so long as a rational person respects himself, that is, so long as he lives as well as he can, his title to the respect of others is complete ...

[The state's] progress, he will recognize, as did a great philosopher, to be 'the coming of the kingdom of heaven upon earth'; and the little services which he contributes to it, at his station, however humble, will have a new value. He finds that through doing the duty of the day he is securing more than his own comfort and the well-being of those who depend upon him: he is building his own character, and at the same time he is a humble hod-bearer on the walls of a greater and far more permanent edifice than his own character: he is building the State.

This sense of one-ness with a great cause, of a unity which is more vital than any copartnership, exalts the value of life beyond all computation. It is one of the secrets of the power of both morality and religion. And a good citizen of a good State has a right to its support, and he does well to foster it by fuller knowledge of the magnitude of his cause. For his life and that of his country *are* one. Neither he nor it *can* live for itself alone. He finds his living personality in the State, and the State finds its personality in him. In his consciousness, up to the measure of his intelligence and will to good, the purposes of the State are formed. He is its eye and ear and thinking soul ...

Nevertheless that the human being, as human, has rights cannot be denied. They are innate, and they are inalienable, and their ground is in the man himself. They are intrinsic. But they are in him as a social being. They belong to him in virtue of the recognition of a common good by the community in which and by which he lives a more or less rational life; and they are the more fully his, the more inalienable and comprehensive, the wider and the fuller the content of that common good. The rights are valid and genuine in the degree to which the citizen, on his part, exercises them in such a way as to develop his best powers with a view to, and therefore in the service of, the common good. The aim of the individual and the State is thus one and the same. The State provides the opportunities, the citizens use these opportunities. To provide the former is the duty of the State and the right of the citizen; to provide the latter, the use, is the duty of the citizen and the right of the State. As the common good is the good of both the State and the individual citizen, both the State and the citizen are ends in themselves.

Sir Henry Jones, *Principles of Citizenship* (London: Macmillan, 1919), pp. 51–3, 56–7, 93, 100, 148.

9. Critical Times

Harold J. Laski 1893–1950

The scale of modern civilisation has of itself done much to deprive the citizen of his freedom. He cannot hope, in populations of the modern size, that his own voice will be clearly heard. To want effectively he must be part of an organisation wide enough and significant enough to be able to make its impress upon political authority. The citizen to-day is lost who stands alone. It is as part of a group that he secures the power to fulfil himself.

But even as a member of a group, citizenship is not necessarily available to him. The more ample the size and functions of the modern State, the less opportunity has the average citizen to take an important share in the disposal of its business. The number of those who can occupy office, whether central or local, is necessarily fractional; and political significance will come to most, as Rousseau saw, only at election time ...

And in a society like our own, the main characteristic of which is economic inequality, it follows that the insistent demand is not that which has the greatest claim to satisfaction, but that which has the greatest economic power behind it. It is the will of this demand which shapes the whole fabric of the State. Inequality at the base breeds inequality at the apex of the social pyramid. The consumer becomes the prisoner of the profit-maker. He must take what he is given. He cannot himself, in a profit-making world, even hope to control the economic process of which he is a part. His wants must fit themselves to what the profit-maker believes will be good for himself. Consumption is not, like production, something of an art. It is an acceptance of enforced alternatives in which profit is visible to the producer. Industry, which should be the servant of the consumer, is, in a context of this kind, his master ...

Anyone who compares the quality of citizenship in ancient Greece with that of our own day cannot help but perceive a certain loss of spiritual energy. And this loss, it may reasonably be argued, is essentially the outcome of our failure to plan our civilisation. We have believed that the mere conflict of private interests will, given liberty of contract, necessarily result in social good; and we have forgotten, because the simplicity of bare political equality obscures the real factors beneath, that liberty of contract is never genuine in the absence of equality of bargaining power. Such equality demands, as its primary condition, the presence of combination ...

The consumer, in fact, has done little or nothing to control his environment. He does not announce his wants; he waits for the profit-maker to discover such of his wants as it is worth his while to supply. But since the quality of his citizenship largely depends upon what there is for him to consume, ignorance of his wants means, in a high degree, the absence of a civic context to this aspect of his life. The things he purchases do not come to him as part of a process deliberately conceived to enlarge his personality...

For the modern State the central problem is the capacity to satisfy demand...

A State, after all, is no mystic institution. It is a body of men and women who search for self-realisation and admit in a particular association an especially majestic power that the hindrances to its achievement, whether positive or negative, may be removed. The business of the State is therefore dependent upon its power to maintain a condition of liberty and equality. It needs the first lest barriers operate to prevent the emergence of that continuous initiative upon which self-realisation depends. It needs the second because unless it is admitted that the interests of each citizen in self-realisation are identical (however various be the modes of its expression), it is inevitable that the many will become the instruments of the few instead of being regarded as ends in themselves. And this is the definition of slavery.

It was the perception that human beings are ends in themselves, entitled equally to self-realisation, which has been the driving-power behind the movement towards political democracy. With the coming of universal suffrage, the abolition, further, of political discrimination against creed or class or race in its power to be chosen for positions of authority, it has seemed to many that the central problem of the State has been solved. Yet no one can survey the post-war world and hold, for one moment, that there is ground for effective satisfaction ...

We shall not make citizenship a tangible and adequate reality until we make the demand of the average man both organised and coherent. We shall not achieve this end save by the discovery of methods of social organisation which emphasise the equality of their claim upon the common stock and apportion that stock in such fashion as to leave by its distribution the maximum possible satisfaction. It is difficult to suppose – at least in the light of experience – that this is possible in a world which, like our own, places its reliance upon profit and competition as the sources of social well-being...

To trust to individual self-interest as the mainspring of social effort is not merely to postpone, but actually to defeat, the prospect of a common good. Yet when we come to the consideration of other possibilities, wisdom consists not in the search for a panacea, but in the discovery of methods of organisation which adapt the service we require through means most likely to secure the maximum of social benefit in the result ...

What, to that end, modern democracy needs is the revelation of an alternative social philosophy which will do for the new social order what

Adam Smith and Bentham did for the old. In a society like that of the eighteenth century, there was solid ground for insisting on the supreme benefit of free competition and individual initiative as the main weapons against an effete aristocracy and an indefensible privilege. But what has emerged from an experience of individualism is the fact that free competition and individual initiative merely create new aristocracies and new privileges as unnecessary and as indefensible as the old. The cause of this is plain. When the profit-making motive is the mainspring of social action, its operation is incompatible with democracy. For the liberty it establishes is biased in favour of those who can establish by their skill in its use a differential advantage in their favour; and this advantage, on the evidence, is mainly purchased at the cost of the community as a whole. What we require is a philosophy which prevents that differential advantage from preventing the expression of the equal claim of citizens to self-realisation. We need, in other words, an equality which can evoke from men those demands which cannot go unsatisfied if the inherent dignity of their manhood is to secure satisfaction ...

Not since the fall of the Roman Empire has the principle of Western civilisation been in graver danger than in our own day. The predominance of capitalist imperialism means inevitably, with an awakening East, the prospect of ultimate disaster. Conflicts of race and colour, the challenge to the march of reason by men avid for power and impatient of the slow process of persuasion, the danger of creed wars – these confront us on every hand. They are stimulated and quickened by the profit-making motive as by a poison which drives men recklessly to the abyss. Democracy depends on the willingness of the individual citizen to use his instructed judgment for the public good.

Harold J. Laski, *The Recovery of Citizenship* (London: Ernest Benn, 1928), pp. 3, 4–5, 6, 7, 10–11, 12–13, 20–1, 28.

10. The Typical Citizen is a Primitive

Joseph A. Schumpeter 1883–1946

... there are many national issues that concern individuals and groups so directly and unmistakably as to evoke volitions that are genuine and definite enough. The most important instance is afforded by issues involving immediate and personal pecuniary profit to individual voters and groups of voters, such as direct payments, protective duties, silver policies and so on. Experience that goes back to antiquity shows that by and large voters react promptly and rationally to any such chance. But the classical doctrine of democracy evidently stands to gain little from displays of rationality of this kind. Voters thereby prove themselves bad and indeed corrupt judges of such issues, and often they even prove themselves bad judges of their own long-run interests, for it is only the short-run promise that tells politically and only short-run rationality that asserts itself effectively.

However, when we move still farther away from the private concerns of the family and the business office into those regions of national and international affairs that lack a direct and unmistakable link with those private concerns, individual volition, command of facts and method of inference soon cease to fulfill the requirements of the classical doctrine. What strikes me most of all and seems to me to be the core of the trouble is the fact that the sense of reality is so completely lost. Normally, the great political questions take their place in the psychic economy of the typical citizen with those leisure-hour interests that have not attained the rank of hobbies, and with the subjects of irresponsible conversation. These things seem so far off; they are not at all like a business proposition; dangers may not materialize at all and if they should they may not prove so very serious; one feels oneself to be moving in a fictitious world.

This reduced sense of reality accounts not only for a reduced sense of responsibility but also for the absence of effective volition. One has one's phrases, of course, and one's wishes and daydreams and grumbles: especially, one has one's likes and dislikes. But ordinarily they do not amount to what we call a will – the psychic counterpart of purposeful responsible action. In fact, for the private citizen musing over national affairs there is no scope for such a will and no task at which it could develop. He is a member of an unworkable committee, the committee of the whole nation, and this is why he expends less disciplined effort on mastering a political problem than he expends on a game of bridge.

The reduced sense of responsibility and the absence of effective volition in turn explain the ordinary citizen's ignorance and lack of judgment in matters of domestic and foreign policy which are if anything more shocking in the case of educated people and of people who are successfully active in non-political walks of life than it is with uneducated people in humble stations. Information is plentiful and readily available. But this does not seem to make any difference.

... the typical citizen drops down to a lower level of mental performance as soon as he enters the political field. He argues and analyzes in a way which he would readily recognize as infantile within the sphere of his real interests. He becomes a primitive again. His thinking becomes associative and affective. And this entails two further consequences of ominous significance.

First, even if there were no political groups trying to influence him, the typical citizen would in political matters tend to yield to extra-rational or irrational prejudice and impulse. The weakness of the rational processes he applies to politics and the absence of effective logical control over the results he arrives at would in themselves suffice to account for that. Moreover, simply because he is not 'all there,' he will relax his usual moral standards as well and occasionally give in to dark urges which the conditions of private life help him to repress. But as to the wisdom or rationality of his inferences and conclusions, it may be just as bad if he gives in to a burst of generous indignation. This will make it still more difficult for him to see things in their correct proportions or even to see more than one aspect of one thing at a time. Hence, if for once he does emerge from his usual vagueness and does display the definite will postulated by the classical doctrine of democracy, he is as likely as not to become still more unintelligent and irresponsible than he usually is. At certain junctures, this may prove fatal to his nation.

Second, however, the weaker the logical element in the processes of the public mind and the more complete the absence of rational criticism and of the rationalizing influence of personal experience and responsibility, the greater are the opportunities for groups with an axe to grind. These groups may consist of professional politicians or of exponents of an economic interest or of idealists of one kind or another or of people simply interested in staging and managing political shows. The sociology of such groups is immaterial to the argument in hand. The only point that matters here is that, Human Nature in Politics being what it is, they are able to fashion and, within very wide limits, even to create the will of the people. What we are confronted with in the analysis of political processes is largely not a genuine but a manufactured will. And often this artefact is all that in reality corresponds to the *volonté générale* of the classical doctrine. So far as this is so, the will of the people is the product and not the motive power of the political process ...

We have seen above why it is so difficult to impart to the public unbiased information about political problems and logically correct inferences from it and why it is that information and arguments in political matters will 'register' only if they link up with the citizen's preconceived ideas. As a rule, however, these ideas are not definite enough to determine particular conclusions. Since they can themselves be manufactured, effective political argument almost inevitably implies the attempt to twist existing volitional premises into a particular shape and not merely the attempt to implement them or to help the citizen to make up his mind ...

There are of course limits to all this. And there is truth in Jefferson's dictum that in the end the people are wiser than any single individual can be, or in Lincoln's about the impossibility of 'fooling all the people all the time.' But both dicta stress the long-run aspect in a highly significant way. It is no doubt possible to argue that given time the collective psyche will evolve opinions that not infrequently strike us as highly reasonable and even shrewd. History however consists of a succession of short-run situations that may alter the course of events for good. If all the people can in the short run be 'fooled' step by step into something they do not really want, and if this is not an exceptional case which we could afford to neglect, then no amount of retrospective common sense will alter the fact that in reality they neither raise or decide issues but that the issues that shape their fate are normally raised and decided for them. More than anyone else the lover of democracy has every reason to accept this fact and to clear his creed from the aspersion that it rests upon make-believe.

Joseph A. Schumpeter, *Capitalism, Socialism and Democracy* (London: George Allen and Unwin, 1943), pp. 260–4.

11. Class and Citizenship

T.H. Marshall 1893–1981

Is it still true that basic equality, when enriched in substance and embodied in the formal rights of citizenship, is consistent with the inequalities of social class? I shall suggest that our society today assumes that the two are still compatible, so much so that citizenship has itself become, in certain respects, the architect of legitimate social inequality...

I propose to divide citizenship into three parts. But the analysis is, in this case, dictated by history even more clearly than by logic. I shall call these three parts, or elements, civil, political and social. The civil element is composed of the rights necessary for individual freedom – liberty of the person, freedom of speech, thought and faith, the right to own property and to conclude valid contracts, and the right to justice. The last is of a different order from the others, because it is the right to defend and assert all one's rights on terms of equality with others and by due process of law. This shows us that the institutions most directly associated with civil rights are the courts of justice. By the political element I mean the right to participate in the exercise of political power, as a member of a body invested with political authority or as an elector of the members of such a body. The corresponding institutions are parliament and councils of local government. By the social element I mean the whole range from the right to a modicum of economic welfare and security to the right to share to the full in the social heritage and to live the life of a civilized being according to the standards prevailing in the society. The institutions most closely connected with it are the educational system and the social services.

In early times these three strands were wound into a single thread. There rights were blended because the institutions were amalgamated...

When the three elements of citizenship parted company, they were soon barely on speaking terms. So complete was the divorce between them that it is possible, without doing too much violence to historical accuracy, to assign the formative period in the life of each to a different century – civil rights to the eighteenth, political to the nineteenth and social to the twentieth. These periods must, of course, be treated with reasonable elasticity, and there is some evident overlap, especially between he last two ...

In the economic field the basic civil right is the right to work, that is to say the right to follow the occupation of one's choice in the place of one's choice, subject only to legitimate demands for preliminary technical training ...

The story of political rights is different both in time and in character. The formative period began, as I have said, in the early nineteenth century, when the civil rights attached to the status of freedom had already acquired sufficient substance to justify us in speaking of a general status of citizenship. And, when it began, it consisted, not in the creation of new rights to enrich a status already enjoyed by all, but in the granting of old rights to new sections of the population ...

The original source of social rights was membership of local communities and functional associations. This source was supplemented and progressively replaced by a Poor Law and a system of wage regulation which were nationally conceived and locally administered ...

The education of children has a direct bearing on citizenship, and, when the State guarantees that all children shall be educated, it has the requirements and the nature of citizenship definitely in mind. It is trying to stimulate the growth of citizens in the making. The right to education is a genuine social right of citizenship, because the aim of education during childhood is to shape the future adult. Fundamentally it should be regarded, not as the right of the child to go to school, but as the right of the adult citizen to have been educated. And there is here no conflict with civil rights as interpreted in an age of individualism. For civil rights are designed for use by reasonable and intelligent persons, who have learned to read and write. Education is a necessary prerequisite of civil freedom.

But, by the end of the nineteenth century, elementary education was not only free, it was compulsory. This signal departure from *laissez faire* could, of course, be justified on the grounds that free choice is a right only for mature minds, that children are naturally subject to discipline, and that parents cannot be trusted to do what is in the best interests of their children. But the principle goes deeper than that. We have here a personal right combined with a public duty to exercise the right. Is the public duty imposed merely for the benefit of the individual – because children cannot fully appreciate their own interests and parents may be unfit to enlighten them? I hardly think that this can be an adequate explanation. It was increasingly recognized, as the nineteenth century wore on, that political democracy needed an educated electorate, and that scientific manufacture needed educated workers and technicians. The duty to improve and civilize oneself is therefore a social duty, and not merely a personal one, because the social health of a society depends upon the civilization of its members. And a community that enforces this duty has begun to realize that its culture is an organic unity and its civilization a national heritage. It follows that the growth of public elementary education during the nineteenth century was the first decisive step on the road to the re-establishment of the social rights of citizenship in the twentieth ...

Citizenship is a status bestowed on those who are full members of a community. All who possess the status are equal with respect to the rights and duties with which the status is endowed. There is no universal principle that determines what those rights and duties shall be, but societies in which citizenship is a developing institution create an image of an ideal citizenship against which achievement can be measured and towards which aspiration can be directed. The urge forward along the path thus plotted is an urge towards a fuller measure of equality, an enrichment of the stuff of which the status is made and an increase in the number of those on whom the status is bestowed. Social class, on the other hand, is a system of inequality. And it too, like citizenship, can be based on a set of ideals, beliefs and values. It is therefore reasonable to expect that the impact of citizenship on social class should take the form of a conflict between opposing principles. If I am right in my contention that citizenship has been a developing institution in England at least since the latter part of the seventeenth century, then it is clear that its growth coincides with the rise of capitalism, which is a system, not of equality, but of inequality. Here is something that needs explaining. How is it that these two opposing principles could grow and flourish side by side in the same soil? What made it possible for them to be reconciled with one another and to become, for a time at least, allies instead of antagonists? The question is a pertinent one, for it is clear that, in the twentieth century, citizenship and the capitalist class system have been at war ...

The equality implicit in the concept of citizenship, even though limited in content, undermined the inequality of the class system, which was in principle a total inequality. National justice and a law common to all must inevitably weaken and eventually destroy class justice, and personal freedom, as a universal birthright, must drive out serfdom. No subtle argument is needed to show that citizenship is incompatible with medieval feudalism...

The components of a civilized and cultured life, formerly the monopoly of the few, were brought progressively within reach of the many, who were encouraged thereby to stretch out their hands towards those that still eluded their grasp. The diminution of inequality strengthened the demand for its abolition, at least with regard to the essentials of social welfare.

These aspirations have in part been met by incorporating social rights in the status of citizenship and thus creating a universal right to real income which is not proportionate to the market value of the claimant. Class-abatement is still the aim of social rights, but it has acquired a new meaning. It is no longer merely an attempt to abate the obvious nuisance of destitution in the lowest ranks of society. It has assumed the guise of action modifying the whole pattern of social inequality. It is no longer content to raise the floor-level in the basement of the social edifice, leaving the superstructure as it was. It has begun to remodel the whole building, and it might even end by converting a skyscraper into a bungalow. It is therefore important to consider whether any such ultimate aim is implicit in the nature of this development, or whether, as I put it at the outset, there are natural limits to the contemporary drive towards greater social and economic equality ...

I see no signs of any relaxation of the bonds that tie education to occupation. On the contrary, they appear to be growing stronger. Great and increasing respect is paid to certificates, matriculation, degrees and diplomas as qualifications for employment, and their freshness does not fade with the passage of the years ...

The right of the citizen in this process of selection and mobility is the right to equality of opportunity. Its aim is to eliminate hereditary privilege. In essence it is the equal right to display and develop differences, or inequalities; the equal right to be recognized as unequal. In the early stages of the establishment of such a system the major effect is, of course, to reveal hidden equalities – to enable the poor boy to show that he is as good as the rich boy. But the final outcome is a structure of unequal status fairly apportioned to unequal abilities ...

The conclusion of importance to my argument is that, through education in its relations with occupational structure, citizenship operates as an instrument of social stratification. There is no reason to deplore this, but we should be aware of its consequences. The status acquired by education is carried out into the world bearing the stamp of legitimacy, because it has been conferred by an institution designed to give the citizen his just rights. That which the market offers can be measured against that which the status claims. If a large discrepancy appears, the ensuing attempts to eliminate it will take the form, not of a bargain about economic value, but of a debate about social rights ...

If citizenship is invoked in the defence of rights, the corresponding duties of citizenship cannot be ignored. These do not require a man to sacrifice his individual liberty or to submit without question to every demand made by government. But they do require that his acts should be inspired by a lively sense of responsibility towards the welfare of the community.

T.H. Marshall, 'Citizenship and Social Class' [1950], in T.H. Marshall, *Citizenship and Social Class and Other Essays* (London: Pluto Press, 1991) pp. 7, 8, 10, 12, 14, 16–19, 28, 38–41.

12. What is the Good Citizen?

Gabriel A. Almond and Sidney Verba

The citizen, unlike the subject, is an active participant in the political input process – the process by which political decisions are made. But the citizen role does not replace the subject role or the parochial role: it is added to them. Only the rare individual considers his role as citizen more important and salient than his role as subject or parochial, for whom politics is a matter of first priority. This has been corroborated in many surveys of political opinion. When asked general questions about what worries them, or what they consider important, people usually mention family problems, job problems, economic problems, but rarely political problems. Furthermore, if the ordinary man is interested in political matters, he is more likely to be interested in the output than in the input process. He is concerned about who wins the election, not about how it is carried on; he cares about who is benefited by legislation, not about how legislation is passed. Even in relation to his vote – an act that is designed to make him an active participant in the decision-making processes of his nation – he may behave routinely, voting for a party because of traditional allegiance or for other reasons not connected with a desire to guide the course of policy.

That most men orient themselves more as subjects than as citizens is a familiar theme. Much has been written describing this fact, sometimes deploring it. Interest in and criticism of the role of the ordinary man in his political system is especially characteristic of those writers and thinkers concerned with the problems of democracy – from the ancient Greeks to current writers on American civic affairs; for it is in a democracy that the role of the ordinary man as a participant in the political affairs of his country is significant. The man whose relation to his government is that of a subject – a passive beneficiary or victim of routine governmental actions – would not be found wanting in a traditional, nondemocratic society. Moreover, this relationship would exhaust what is expected of him. What the government does affects him, but why or how the government decides to do what it does is outside his sphere of competence. He has obligations, but the obligations are passive – he should be loyal and respectful of authority. 'All that is necessary for salvation is contained in two virtues, *faith* in Christ and *obedience* to law.' As a subject he may be more or less competent, but his competence will be 'subject competence.' He will not attempt to influence the decisions of his government, but will try to see that he is treated properly once the decision is made. It is not in his sphere of competence to say what taxes should be levied, but once these are decided the competent subject will see that he is treated fairly within the boundaries of that decision. The law is something he obeys, not something he helps shape. If he is competent, he knows the law, knows what he must do, and what is due him.

In democratic societies, on the other hand, his role as subject does not exhaust what is expected of him. He is expected to have the virtues of the subject – to obey the law, to be loyal – but he is also expected to take some part in the formation of decisions. The common thread running through the many definitions of democracy is that a democracy is a society in which '... ordinary citizens exert a relatively high degree of control over leaders.' Democracy is thus characterized by the fact that power over significant authoritative decisions in a society is distributed among the population. The ordinary man is expected to take an active part in governmental affairs, to be aware of how decisions are made, and to make his views known.

The fact that the ordinary man does not live up to the ideal set by the normative theory of democracy has led to much criticism of his passivity and indifference. Our goal is to describe and analyze, however, and not to assign praise or blame. In any case, normative questions about the role of the individual in his political system are by no means unrelated to more descriptive and analytic questions. Certainly the political moralist in describing what an individual *should* do will probably not be unaffected by what individuals actually *do*, and certainly he will consider what he believes that *can* do. The three types of questions are not identical, but they affect one another, especially if we switch our perspective to that of the ordinary man himself. So far we have talked about the gap between what scholars, philosophers, and teachers have said the ordinary man ought to do in a democracy and what in fact he does. But what about the ordinary man himself? What does *he* think he *should* do? And how does this compare with what he thinks he *can* do and with what he does?

This selection will deal with the first question: What does the ordinary man think he should do? Philosophers and democratic ideologists have written at length about the obligations of the citizen, but what is the ordinary man's conception of his role in politics? If the model democratic citizen is active, participating, and influential, is this what the ordinary man aspires to be? And, what may be more important, does he think of himself as capable of influencing and participating in the decisions of his government?

What is the Good Citizen?

The good citizen does not equal the good man. No zealous advocate of good citizenship would argue that political participation ought to be pursued to the neglect of all other obligations. The active influential citizen described in normative political theory is not excused from the obligations of the subject. If he participates in the making of the law, he is also expected to obey the law. It has, in fact, been argued that he has greater obligation to obey because of his participation. Nor would one want his civic activity to be at the expense of his private obligations. Surely the lady described by Riesman who left her screaming children locked in their room while she attended a meeting of a neighborhood improvement association does not represent the ideal toward which the advocates of good citizenship are striving. There will, of course, always be conflicts between the demands of different roles, but the obligations of one role do not replace those of another.

This point is stressed here because it introduces a complexity into our attempt to measure the extent to which the ideal of the participating citizen exists in the minds of men; for the man who believes that he should be upright in his personal life – work for the good of his family or, to quote one of our respondents, 'If he is a carpenter, he should be a good carpenter' – may also believe that he should be a participating and active citizen. Similarly, the man who believes that he should pay taxes and obey the laws is a 'good subject.' The same man may also be a 'good citizen.' It is only when the individual thinks of his family's advantage as the only goal to pursue, or conceives of his role in the political system in familistic terms, that he is a parochial and not also a citizen. And it is only when an individual thinks of his relationship to his state as being exhausted by his role as subject that he is subject and not also citizen.

Attempting to see how much the role of participant has been added to those of parochial and subject in our five countries, we examined our respondents' relationships with their local community. We were interested in the extent to which respondents considered themselves to have some sort of responsibility to be active in their community – either in a formal or an informal way; either in relation to local government or in relation to fellow citizens. The local community seemed to be a good place to begin, since political and governmental problems tend to be more understandable, the organs of government less distant, the chances of effective participation for the individual citizen greater on the local level than on the level of national government. In fact, it has often been argued that effective democracy rests on the ability of the individual to participate locally, for it is only here that he can develop some sense of mastery over political affairs. As Bryce put it (and as defenders of local autonomy have constantly argued), 'An essential ingredient of a satisfactory democracy is that a considerable proportion should have experience of active participation in the work of small self-governing groups, whether in connection with local government, trade unions, cooperatives or other forms of activity.'

Reprinted by permission of Sage Publications Inc, Gabriel A. Almond and Sidney Verba, *The Civic Culture* (New York: Sage, 1991), pp. 117–21.

13. Citizen or Person?

Alexander M. Bickel 1924–74

Special qualifications for naturalization do exist and are enforced. Good moral character is one. However, qualifications that seek to pour ideological and political meaning into the concept of citizenship meet with judicial resistance. Nor has Congress been permitted to define the allegiance of those already citizens by providing for their involuntary expatriation – the involuntary loss of citizenship – upon commission of acts inconsistent with allegiance. Such acts by citizens and even by noncitizens may be punished, but loss of citizenship cannot be predicated on them. And the irony is that in the decisions that denied a power to impose involuntary expatriation and thus seemed to follow the tradition of denuding the concept of citizenship in our law of any special role and content, the Supreme Court returned to a rhetoric of exalting citizenship which echoes the Taney opinion in *Dred Scott*.

In the early years of the Republic, Hamilton and his followers believed that, like British subjects, Americans should be tied indissolubly to the state; a right of voluntary expatriation would encourage subversion. But voluntary expatriation has long been permitted by our law. Jefferson supported such a right, and in the end his view prevailed. In 1868 Congress, having for the first time defined citizenship, passed a statute still on the books providing, in warm language, that 'the right of expatriation is a natural and inherent right of all people, indispensable to the enjoyment of the rights of life, liberty and the pursuit of happiness,' and was not to be denied. We had, after all, fought in 1812 against British claims that immigrants from Great Britain who were sailors in our navy could be treated by the British as deserters because they had never lost their British nationality, and in the 1860s we were indignant at British treatment of naturalized Irish-Americans arrested in Ireland for participation in anti-British activities. [See Charles Gordon, 'The Citizen and the State: Power of Congress to Expatriate American Citizens,' 53 *Georgetown Law Journal* 315 (1965).]

Congress listed as expatriating behavior such acts as voting in a foreign political election or deserting from the armed forces in time of war, or, for a naturalized citizen, taking up permanent residence in the country of his or her birth. In the end the Court held them all unconstitutional (Afroyim v. Rusk, 387 U.S. 253 [1967]: Schneider v. Rusk, 377 U.S. 163 [1964]), although there is some slight evidence that the Court as now constituted might be willing to some extent to rethink the whole question (see Rogers v. Bellei, 401 U.S. 815 [1971]). The Court said, in effect, in these cases holding the involuntary expatriation statutes unconstitutional, that Congress may not put that much content into the concept of citizenship. It seemed to reaffirm the traditional minimal content of the concept of citizenship, the minimal definition of allegiance. But its language was at war with its action. 'This government was born of its citizens,' wrote Chief Justice Earl Warren,

> it maintains itself in a continuing relationship with them, and, in my judgment, it is without power to sever the relationship that gives rise to its existence. I cannot believe that a government conceived in the spirit of ours was established with power to take from the people their most basic right.
>
> Citizenship *is* man's basic right for it is nothing less than the right to have rights. Remove this priceless possession and there remains a stateless person, disgraced and degraded in the eyes of his countrymen. He has no lawful claim to protection from any nation, and no nation may assert rights on his behalf. His very existence is at the sufferance of the state within whose borders he happens to be. [As if our government were in the habit of beheading people for not being citizens!] In this country the expatriate would presumably enjoy, at most, only the limited rights and privileges of aliens ...
>
> The people who created this government endowed it with broad powers ... But the citizens themselves are sovereign, and their citizenship is not subject to the general powers of their government. (Perez v. Brownell, 356 U.S. 44, 64–65 [1957] Warren, Black, and Douglas dissenting.) This dissent within the decade became the prevailing view. The chief justice took his clue from an unguarded comment by Brandeis, made in a quite different context, to the effect that deportation of one who claims to be a citizen may result in the loss of 'all that makes life worth living.' Ng Fung Ho v. White, 259 U.S. 276, 284 (1922).]

Citizenship, Warren concluded, is 'that status, which alone assures the full enjoyment of the precious rights conferred by our Constitution.' Ten years later, when these views came to command a majority [Afroyim v. Rusk, 387 U.S. 253 (1967)], Justice Black wrote: 'In our country the people are sovereign and the Government cannot sever its relationship to the people by taking away their citizenship' [Ibid. at 257]. And: 'Its citizenry is the country and the country is its citizenry' [Ibid. at 268].

All this, as we have seen, is simply not so. It is not so on the face of the Constitution, and it certainly has not been so since the *Slaughter-House Cases* of 1873. The Warren language was a regression to the confusions of Bingham and, what is worse, to the majority opinion in *Dred Scott* v. *Sandford*, which held that the terms 'people of the United States' and 'citizens' are synonymous and that they 'both describe the political body who according to our republican institutions form the sovereignty.' Who said, 'They are what we familiarly call the single "sovereign people," and every citizen is one of this people and a constituent member of the sovereignty'? Roger B. Taney did, and Earl Warren and Hugo L. Black echoed it a century later, unwittingly to be sure. Who said that noncitizens 'had no rights or privileges but such as those who held the power and the government might choose to grant them'? Roger B. Taney, to the same curious later echo.

No matter to what purpose it is put and by whom, this is regressive. Its thrust is parochial and exclusive. A relationship between government and the governed that turns on citizenship can always be dissolved or denied. Citizenship is a legal construct, an abstraction, a theory. No matter what the safeguards, it is at best something given, and given to some and not to others, and it can be taken away. It has always been easier, it always will be easier, to think of someone as a noncitizen than to decide that he is a nonperson, which is the point of the *Dred Scott* case. Emphasis on citizenship as the tie that binds the individual to government and as the source of his rights leads to metaphysical thinking about politics and law, and more particularly to symmetrical thinking, to a search for reciprocity and symmetry and clarity of uncompromised rights and obligations, rationally ranged one next and against the other. Such thinking bodes ill for the endurance of free, flexible, responsive, and stable institutions and of a balance between order and liberty. It is by such thinking, as in Rousseau's *The Social Contract*, that the claims of liberty may be readily translated into the postulates of oppression. I find it gratifying, therefore, that we live under a Constitution to which the concept of citizenship matters very little, that prescribes decencies and wise modalities of government quite without regard to the concept of citizenship. It subsumes important obligations and functions of the individual which have other sources – moral, political, and traditional – sources more complex than the simple contractarian notion of citizenship. 'The simple governments,' wrote Burke, 'are fundamentally defective, to say no worse of them.' Citizenship is at best a simple idea for a simple government.

Alexander M. Bickel, 'Citizen or Person? What Is Not Granted Cannot Be Taken Away', ch. 2 in *The Morality of Consent* (London: Yale University Press, 1975), pp. 50–4. Copyright 1975 in the estate of Alexander M. Bickel. Reproduced by kind permission of Yale University Press.

14. Citizenship and Capitalism

Bryan Turner

Citizenship may be defined in a variety of ways (by reference to civil, legal and social features) but citizenship rights are essentially concerned with the nature of social participation of persons within the community as fully recognized legal members. Citizenship expands with the boundaries which contain society so that the more limited the nature of society the more limited the nature of citizenship rights ...

Citizenship is a radical and socially disruptive process whereby, through a series of expanding processes, social membership becomes increasingly universalistic and open-ended.

The movement of citizenship is from the particular to the universal, since particular definitions of persons for the purpose of exclusion appear increasingly irrational and incongruent with the basis of the modern polity. The expansion of citizenship is from ascription to achievement. The development of citizenship is also from the hierarchical to the horizontal, so that fixed positions of a formal status system begin to dissolve under the impact of universalistic democratic rights of citizenship. It is for this reason that citizenship provides us with a measure of modernization, where modernization involves the collapse of legitimate systems of patriarchy, gerontocracy and patrimonialism. These hierarchical structures are replaced by naked competition in the market place where classes and other occupational groups seek through exclusionary practices to preserve their privileged access to resources. These market practices are also subject to criticism from democratic citizenship where forms of positive discrimination are mobilized to seek a redress between advantaged and disadvantaged groups. The growth of modernity is a movement from de-jure inequalities in terms of legitimate status hierarchies to de-facto inequalities as a consequence of naked market forces where the labourer is defined as a 'free' person ...

Whether or not citizenship provides the ultimate institutional support for the continuity of capitalism is primarily an empirical question which should be addressed by sociological research rather than being specified in advance. However, it seems perfectly plausible to believe that citizenship (especially in terms of civil and legal rights) supports the continuity of the capitalist mode of production by giving expression to bourgeois requirements in the market place and also that citizenship supports capitalism in the sense of providing some form of abatement of direct conflict between groups. This position is perfectly in line with Marshall's view of the role of such bourgeois freedoms as the right to own property. However, we can also argue that citizenship undermines the capacity of private capitalist enterprises to realize their investment through profits since the expansion of social rights is translated into increased taxation, state regulation of the market and legislation to control the inheritance of property ...

All social institutions have contradictory consequences. It is neither the case that citizenship always supports the stability of capitalism, nor that it inevitably undermines it ...

Although capitalism is inherently violent and exploitative, it creates a context in which progressive forces may develop and where an enhancement of human reason and experience becomes possible. Citizenship exists despite rather than because of capitalist growth. The autonomy of the market (despite the relative nature of that autonomy) from culture, social structure and politics creates a space where individualism, universalism, contractual relationships and secularity can develop. The ideological defence of this market by the bourgeoisie against feudal powers in terms of an ideology of property rights was ultimately turned against the bourgeoisie by working classes which mobilized bourgeois culture in defence of equal social rights and the benefits of welfare. Capitalism creates the condition for its own demise and transcendence in that the conditions for socialism grow out of the struggle for genuine rights in capitalism. The anarchy of the market place creates the conditions for the development of the state as that institution which guarantees social contracts and provides an administration within which profits can be realized but the state also becomes an institution necessary for the protection and development of social rights. Capitalism is transformed by a set of institutions which were designed to maintain and protect its continuity. The state in capitalist society is popular rather than bourgeois in the sense that the state arises from popular conflict and struggle to enlarge and democratize state institutions against the interests of capital. The classical Marxist question (namely, why the working classes are not revolutionary) is inadequately posed (Urry, 1981). The Marxist commentary on reformism assumes that capitalist societies have remained largely unchanged and that, since these societies are still capitalist, the proletariat should be revolutionary. However, capitalism has changed at least partly as a result of popular working-class conflict and continues to change as a result of the social struggles of a variety of social movements which are not class-based.

Bryan Turner, *Citizenship and Capitalism* (London: Unwin Hyman, 1985), pp. 134, 135–6, 137, 141–2.

15. Democratic Citizenship

Raymond Plant

A citizenship approach is not new for Labour. Indeed, the theme was taken up in the Party's earliest days, reflecting the impact of Social Liberalism. It is the argument of this pamphlet that this tradition is in urgent need of rethinking and updating much as the modern Conservative Party has rethought the tradition of classical liberalism.

The other main strand of opinion in the early years of the Labour Party, reflecting the Marxist tradition, emphasised a class-based strategy. The class-based approach sees the market as inherently capitalist and its relationships as exploitative and dehumanising.

This clashed with the citizenship approach which assumes that there are common values between different groups and classes in society which are genuine (ie not the product of what Marxists would call false consciousness). These values can provide a basis for political action to secure the rights and resources of citizenship within a mixed economy with some degree of private ownership. The citizenship approach rejects Marx's argument that since class determines political interests there can be no common basis for citizenship while there is some private ownership of the means of production and associated class divisions.

The class approach sees a sense of solidarity and common purpose among members of the class as a necessary prerequisite for the fundamental transformation of society which alone will end exploitation and bring about socialism. The citizenship approach is much more at home with individualism: it sees citizenship as securing the framework of rights and resources within which individuals can pursue their own conception of the good in their own way; and the communal basis of society is reflected in agreement about the common resources and means of citizenship rather than in terms of common ends ...

It is the argument of this pamphlet that the idea of democratic citizenship is the only basis on which Labour can hope to reach a value consensus to determine the broad boundaries of government responsibility and within these to separate legitimate from illegitimate claims. Citizenship embodies a concept of the common good which appeals not to highly specific and sectional goals, but to a set of needs, rights, resources and opportunities which all individuals must have to pursue any goals at all in our sort of society. Such an underlying idea will also indicate the forms of collective and communal provision which are necessary to provide these and the respective roles of the market and the state ...

Citizenship involves negative rights such as rights to be free from

coercion, interference, assault, freedom of expression and association –
all in effect traditional civil and political rights. These are usually
regarded as negative rights since the corresponding obligation on others
is to refrain from assaulting, interfering and coercing. However, as we
saw earlier, the goods of citizenship have to go beyond civil and political
rights and embrace rights to resources, income, health care, education
and welfare. These are usually called positive rights in the sense that
they involve a claim on the resources of others through the tax system.

This latter view of rights and entitlement is firmly rejected by the
New Right arguing that positive rights are rights to resources which are
in themselves scarce and cannot therefore be considered to be objects of
rights. Claims to civil and political rights, because they are rights to be
free from interferences of various sorts, do not involve direct claims to
resources in the way that positive rights do. Indeed, the New Right
asserts that only civil and political rights are genuine rights of citizenship whereas economic and social rights are not.

Of course social and economic rights are asserted against a background of scarce resources, but the contrast between civil and political
rights on the one hand and welfare rights on the other is not as clear-cut as
is suggested ...

The right will also argue that since welfare rights imply resources,
they must infringe property rights, an illegitimate interference with the
property holder's rights to use his property as he or she pleases.
However, all forms of rights including property rights infringe freedom.
Taking property rights as given in our society in which there are
virtually no unowned resources restricts the freedom of non-property
owners to exercise their liberty. Hence, the real question is not about
the infringement of liberty. The question is rather whether, for example,
the right to the means to life has priority over the unfettered right to
property. For the socialist the answer will be clear. However, we should
not succumb to the liberal suggestion that this is an undifferentiated
infringement of liberty.

I now want to look at the question of enforcement, particularly in
relation to welfare rights where the problem is thought to be more
troublesome. This is not to say that the ways in which civil and political
rights are to be protected are unimportant, far from it given the growth
of arbitrary actions by government. However, in this field, the issues
such as whether there should be a Bill of Rights are well understood
and have been quite extensively discussed. The issue of enforcement in
the welfare field, however, is more intractable.

The critic will argue that social and economic rights are not genuine
because they are not justiciable, ie cannot be enforced in law. The
example of the recent litigation over young children requiring heart

operations in Birmingham would support this view. There the judges argued that they could not interfere with clinical judgment in relation to waiting lists.

However, there are alternatives to this model of enforcement. The first would come closest to the justiciable one and argue that although a judge may not be able to enforce a particular right to a specific form of treatment, he does have a role in determining whether a patient's interests have been fully taken into account and that his or her plight is not the result of negligence or inadvertence. So there could be a place for judicial review in this narrower sense. This is not as novel as it looks and applies to a civil right such as equal protection before the law. While a judge cannot dictate the policing policy in a particular city there have been cases where individuals have taken their grievances about policing to court and the question of whether those individuals' interests have been properly taken into account is one to which a judge can address himself. This is not different from the welfare case: the deployment of scarce resources requires professional judgment, but the professional has an obligation to make sure that all interests are properly weighed ...

If rights are to provide a basis for individuals to lead a secure and autonomous life then institutions must themselves enhance this autonomy. Too often the institutions of the welfare state and the growth of professionalism within them has actually led to a reduction in the capacity of individuals for choice and judgment. I doubt whether there is a real way forward in the welfare field without empowering individuals through cash, rights, entitlements and cash surrogates such as vouchers. This is particularly important when the state is effectively the monopoly provider of services in health and welfare for the vast majority of citizens. If they are denied exit either through lack of resources or because the private sector has been removed, then the democratic voice must be increased drastically if we are to be responsive to the idea that citizenship, individual freedom and personal responsibility go together ...

The idea of democratic citizenship is a profoundly anti-capitalist one: it embodies the idea that individuals have a status and a worth to be backed by rights, resources and opportunities which is not determined by their status in the market and their economic value. The underwriting of these rights of citizenship requires collective action and politically guaranteed provision outside the market.

Nevertheless, the economic market is a very useful and indeed central instrument for securing socialist aims ...

So the market itself needs a framework of civic responsibility within which to operate just as interest groups and unions do. Unless such a civic vision is articulated and defended, not just as a matter of altruism but as fall victim to strong special interests whether in politics or in markets. In its claims about the centrality of citizenship and the sense of belonging, the Labour Party is in a better position to defend the range of values which are essential to human life – including self-interest – in a way that the Conservative Party used to do before the accountants took over.

So markets have a central role to play within a socialist society. But they must operate within a set of community values where outcomes will not be regarded as impersonal visitations but adjusted within a frame-work of social justice. As such the market can play a central role in promoting the efficient production of resources without which the ideal of democratic citizenship involving resources, liberties, rights and oppor-tunities will be impossible ...

The aims I have suggested are of an enabling kind. In the context of community it is not the function of public policy to try to create a specific form of community for the whole of society whatever conserva-tives of the left and the right might think. There are profound totalitar-ian dangers in that. Our natures are too diverse to fit into a single pattern of life. We should, however, seek to enable people to form and sustain, where they already exist, their own forms of community which meet their needs. To do this we do need some general community spirit to sustain collective provision, but this only needs to be modest. The idea of community is beguiling but as a general idea and as a guide to policy almost wholly indefinite. People create and sustain their own forms of community, not to have them imposed upon them. Given the resources, a society of citizens, rather than individuals or subjects would be able to form their own communities, as indeed they did in the early years of the socialist movement.

Raymond Plant, *Citizenship, Rights and Socialism*, Fabian Tract no. 531 (London: Fabian Society, October 1988), pp. 1, 3, 10–11, 12, 13, 16, 19, 20.

16. A Citizen of the European Union

Treaty on European Union signed at Maastricht, 7 February 1992

Article A

By this Treaty, the High Contracting Parties establish among themselves a European Union, hereinafter called 'the Union'.

This Treaty marks a new stage in the process of creating an ever closer union among the peoples of Europe, in which decisions are taken as closely as possible to the citizen.

The Union shall be founded on the European Communities, supplemented by the policies and forms of cooperation established by this Treaty. Its task shall be to organize, in a manner demonstrating consistency and solidarity, relations between the Member States and between their peoples ...

Article B

The Union shall set itself the following objectives:

to promote economic and social progress which is balanced and sustainable, in particular through the creation of an area without internal frontiers ....

to strengthen the protection of the rights and interests of the nationals of its Member States through the introduction of a citizenship of the Union ....

Part Two Citizenship of the Union

Article 8

1. Citizenship of the Union is hereby established. Every person holding the nationality of a Member State shall be a citizen of the Union.

2. Citizens of the Union shall enjoy the rights conferred by this Treaty and shall be subject to the duties imposed thereby.

Article 8a

1. Every citizen of the Union shall have the right to move and reside freely within the territory of the Member States, subject to the limitations and conditions laid down in this Treaty and by the measures adopted to give it effect.

Article 8b

1. Every citizen of the Union residing in a Member State of which he is not a national shall have the right to vote and to stand as a candidate at municipal elections in the Member State in which he resides, under the same conditions as nationals of that State. This right shall be exercised subject to detailed arrangements to be adopted before 31 December 1994 by the Council, acting unanimously, on a proposal from the Commission and after consulting the European Parliament; these

arrangements may provide for derogations where warranted by problems specific to a Member State.

2. Without prejudice to Article 1 38(3) and to the provisions adopted for its implementation, every citizen of the Union residing in a Member State of which he is not a national shall have the right to vote and to stand as a candidate in elections to the European Parliament in the Member State in which he resides, under the same conditions as nationals of that State. This right shall be exercised subject to detailed arrangements to be adopted before 31 December 1993 by the Council, acting unanimously on a proposal from the Commission and after consulting the European Parliament; these arrangements may provide for derogations where warranted by problems specific to a Member State.

Article 8c

Every citizen of the Union shall, in the territory of a third country in which the Member State of which he is a national is not represented, be entitled to protection by the diplomatic or consular authorities of any Member State, on the same conditions as the nationals of that State ....

Article 8d

Every citizen of the Union shall have the right to petition the European Parliament ... Every citizen of the Union may apply to the Ombudsman established in accordance with Article 1 38e.

Index